What

"This is really one... you are going to want to buy and use!"
Cleo Chaffin, New Book Reviews, USA

"...better than the knife ...direct, sensible and do-able."
Marilis Hornidge, Book Bag, USA

"...designed for our fast-paced lifestyle.... Instruction is simple, clear and thorough."
Centralia Sentinel

"explains how to... naturally relax, unwind, pamper and rejuvenate your way to a nonsurgical facelift."
Frederick Newspost

"I'm 60 years old... I used to have a double chin, sagging cheeks, but since using [Facelift Naturally] they are all gone.... I advise the readers to...get started today. You'll be surprised at the results."
Louise G. Clark, InnerSelf

"Julia Busch... 53... she looks not a day over 25..."
Martin Merzer, The Miami Herald, USA

What readers are saying

"Facelift Naturally really works....
it really worked wonders on my mouth area.
The lines from my nose to my lips and chin are barely there.... Also, my cheek area seems to be plumper."

"...I noticed a marked difference. I can actually reduce the bags under my eyes (they have existed since my teens). My boyfriend enjoys it too.
He says it helps with his sinus problems."

"I noticed little things happening all within a week or so--
my eyes looked fresher, my cheeks perkier..."

"The lip corner that drooped after cosmetic
surgery is now up after only two weeks."

"...in a short time, the wrinkles around the mouth and
eyes seemed to be easing away."

"It takes no time away from a busy schedule and
it is so relaxing."

My friends keep telling me my face looks wonderful since
I've lost weight, but my husband says,
"It's that face lift you've been doing".

I practice my face lift pretty regularly....
my face looks great!"

FACE LIFT
Naturally

The At-Home or Anywhere, Painless, Natural Facelift for Men and Women that Really Works!

Julia M Busch

Orient Paperbacks
DELHI | MUMBAI | HYDERABAD

The purpose of this book is to educate and entertain. It is not the intent of this program to serve in any way whatsoever as a program for self-treatment of medical problems. Medical problems should be brought to the attention of the reader's physician. Any application of the concepts and\or information contained in this program is done solely at the risk and the discretion of the reader.

All rights reserved. No part of this material may be reproduced or transmitted in any form, or by any means electronic or mechanical, including photocopy, recording, or by any information, storage or retrieval system without the written permission of the publisher, **Orient Paperbacks**, except for the inclusion of brief quotations in a review.

www.orientpaperbacks.com

ISBN 81-222-0221-7

1st Published 1998
3rd Printing 2004

Facelift Naturally

© 1993 Text & Illustrations Julia M. Busch
© 1992 Photographs Scherly Busch Photography. Inc., Florida

Published in arrangement with
Anti-Aging Press, Inc., USA

Cover Design by Vision Studio

Published by
Orient Paperbacks
(A Division of Vision Books Pvt. Ltd.)
Madarsa Road, Kashmere Gate, Delhi-110 006

Printed in India at
Rashtra Rachna Printers, Delhi-110 092

Cover Printed at
Ravindra Printing Press, Delhi-110 006

The secret to becoming younger

Dear Reader,

Congratulations on your decision to challenge the process of aging. You have taken an important step toward lifelong personal esteem and social insurance, not to mention the satisfaction of staying young and the fun of being young.

Recently, at a brunch, the cousin of a friend asked, "How come Julia never ages?" My friend replied, "You'll soon find out." She was referring to the knowledge you are holding in your hands.

When you practice the rejuvenating rituals in this book, your youthful juices will begin to flow and your excitement will grow as your fondest dreams become realities. You will see them reflected back at you in the mirror, in the admiring eyes of your family and friends and the envious eyes of some of your acquaintances. You will delight as the years roll away and your face begins to glow. If you are wrinkle-free, and your skin is taut, you can maintain it with this program.

To provide you with the best possible format, illustrations abound and information is presented clearly, thoroughly and logically. Very soon you will be inconspicuously practicing your lift, anytime, anywhere—all movements are within the normal range of everyday motion.

You will be delighted with the technique, the program and, especially, the results. I am very interested in your progress, suggestions and other anti-aging concerns. Please let me know.

Sincerely,

Julia M. Busch
Publisher

P. S.
Write to me in care of: Orient Paperbacks, Madarsa Road, Kashmere Gate. Delhi-110 006. India

How to use this book

Skim the book briefly. Take note of the segments. The total relaxation-rejuvenation program includes everything from the Back of the Neck and Scalp Massage through the Facelift itself and the Bonus Body Points. Practiced in its entirety, you will see the quickest results.

The Facelift is at its best when the Back of the Neck and Scalp Massage is undertaken just prior to the actual lift. Jiffy lifters may choose only the face and neck points as described in the Facelift segment. And for super busy lifters, who just can't take the twenty-something minutes in one block of time, the Facelift can be further divided and practiced in sections during the day. You can lift standing on line at the market, talking on the phone, in the office, in the classroom, walking the dog, in the bedroom or the board room--all movements are in the normal range of motion. No one will notice.

Mini-Lifts have been included for stubborn areas that need a little extra coaxing. These can be used right from the beginning or later as quickies and touchups.

After skimming the book, go to the beginning and don't miss a thing. When teaching, I have always sought to present knowledge in a practical condensed manner without wasting a word. In this book, you are simply guided step-by-step to youthful glowing skin.

Acknowledgments

For your efforts on this project, thank you:

Hollye Davidson for practical and creative support.

Scherley Busch Photography, Inc., Miami, Florida, dynamic and sensitive photography.

Rhondda Edmiston whose original graphic design was translated into the current format, also Bonnie Bennett and Angela Lovett of Mixed Media Graphic Studio, Miami, Florida.

Shirlee Dreyer and Wally Engelhard of Engelhard Printing, Miami for enthusiastic and meticulous work.

Cover model "H" De La Rosa.

Lynn Whittick for patient and loving editing. Gary Winer for patient and gracious computer assistance.

Bernie Sacks, Jan Nathan, Ben Woodworth, Greg Godeck for invaluable practical advice, and many others.

It has been my pleasure.

Contents

1 LADIES AND GENTLEMEN 15
2 HOW TO TOUCH 19
3 WHERE TO TOUCH 21
4 HOW TO PRESS 23
5 BEGINNING THE RITUAL 27
6 NECK & SCALP MASSAGE 29
7 THE FACELIFT 41
8 THE BONUS POINTS 73
9 MINI-LIFTS FOR PROBLEM AREAS 83
10 HINTS FOR A FABULOUS FACE 113
   PERSONAL NOTES 116
   INDEX 117

Illustrations

Get the "Feel" of the Pads   19
Cross Your Fingers "Piggyback"   20
"Little Magic Buttons"   21
Slowly Begin to Press   22
Stop and Hold   22
Release and Touch   22
Back of the Neck and Scalp Points   31
Points 1A - 4A   32 - 33
Direct Pressure   35
Finger Pivoting   35
Circular Motion Massage   36
Pulsating Massage   36
Points 5A - 8A   38 - 39
Massaging the Scalp   40
Facelift Points   42 - 70, 112
The Forehead or Brow Area   47 - 49
The Eye Area   50 - 54
How to Touch Your Eyes   55
The Cheek Area   56 - 59
The Mouth and Chin Area   60 - 62
Additional Channels to the Face & Neck   63 - 70

Bonus Body Points 75 - 81
1B Pit of Stomach 75
2B Elbow Crease 76
3B Hand 77
4B Wrist 78
5B Lumbar Vertebra 79
6B Lumbar Vertebra 80
7B Foot 81

Mini-Lifts 84 - 111
Forehead or Brow 84 - 85
General Eye Lift I 86 - 87
General Eye Lift II 88 - 89
Upper Lid Lift 90 - 91
Area Between the Eyes 92 - 93
Under Eye Lift 94 - 95
Eyes: Outer Corners 96 - 97
Cheek Lift 98 - 99
Upper Lip Lines 100 - 101
Marionette Lines 102 - 103
Nasolabial Folds 104 - 105
Chin Lift 106 - 107
Double Chin and Neck Lift 108 - 111

To
My Mother
Who can look like a breath of spring
Hollye who is a breath of spring
and to all who wish to look young
at any age

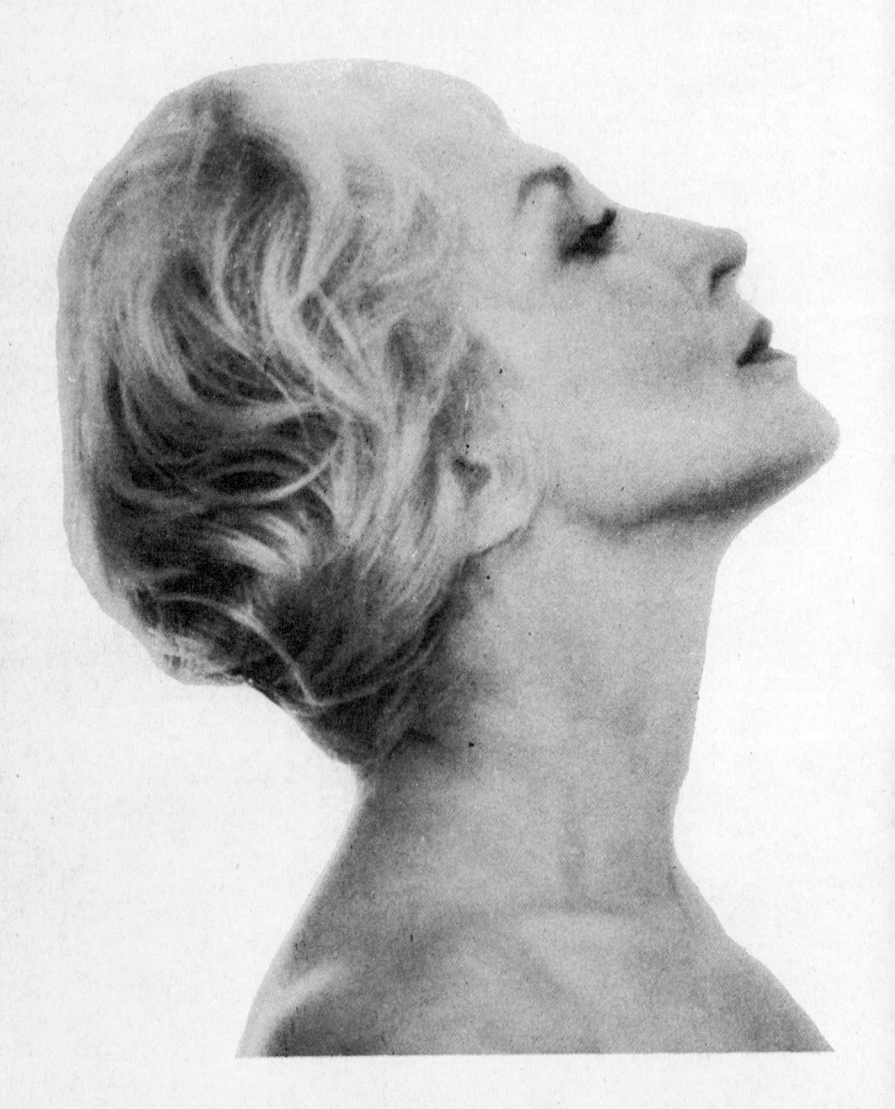

Photographs are unretouched.

1. LADIES & GENTLEMEN

Don't be surprised if by next month you are accused of having had plastic surgery. Such dramatic changes can occur in your face, without pain, without scars and without convalescence. All you need are your hands and the information in these pages. The whole procedure is so easy and takes so little time, it is hard to believe it really works.

If you are beginning to see fine lines they can be eliminated. If your face is beginning to sag, the skin and muscles can be tightened. If your wrinkles are deep it will take a little longer, but you will definitely see results. And, if your skin is still youthful you can keep it that way.

When I began the ritual that I am about to reveal to you amazing things began to happen to me. From the first day, I saw my face relax and begin to glow. After four days, close friends noticed my cheeks plump and the skin around my eyes tighten. The contours on my upper face looked as I remember them 10 years ago. Those "brown spots" began to fade. My skin became softer and smoother. Not only did the wrinkles lighten, they began to disappear. And when I saw the years roll away, I really became excited. My life began to change. I became more hopeful, more outgoing and I even started a publishing company, the Anti-Aging Press, so that I could spread the good news: *You do not have to look old or grow old.* And now... my secret will be yours.

You will stand firm in our youth culture, where we all are judged by appearance in a marketplace that is competitive at any age.

You are about to begin a program that will change your attitude toward the entire process of aging, and very possibly, the program that will change your life.

Rich in its origins, the ritual is based on the mysteries of the ancient Chinese healing art of acupuncture, Japanese Shiatsu pressure techniques, Eastern Do-In manipulations and Western neuromuscular massage. Although it sounds very complex, it is very easy to practice and works very quickly.

In our program, you will, very simply, be using finger pressure that is applied to specific areas. These areas are called pressure points. When a point is pressed, it sends a message over an invisible line called a meridian. The meridian acts very much like a telephone line, transmitting messages of rejuvenation throughout the body. There are many pressure points and many meridians that form an entire systemic network.

Some points are located on your face and head. Others are on your body. But each point has a specific function, and when you press a point on your face, you may feel sensations in other parts of your body as well. Proper pressure on the right points can rebalance your energy and rejuvenate your face and body.

As you proceed with the *Facelift Naturally* program, you may find that headaches disappear, digestion improves, energy increases, your ability to handle stress is enhanced and general body tone and function are better.

A luxury we never seem to have is time, so the program is condensed. A minimal amount of reading gives you the benefit of all the information necessary for self-improvement. The information can be read just once and the technique mastered. Everything is clearly and logically presented, so that in two or three sessions the ritual will be second nature, and the results will simply come.

It's so simple, in fact, that you will be able to "lift" using only one finger while walking the dog, sitting at a stoplight, talking on the phone, on your lunch or coffee break, even in the office or in any public place.

So, are you ready? There are only two things that you must know to accomplish your facelift. One is the location of the pressure points. The other is how to touch and press them. Both are very important.

2. HOW TO TOUCH

When you touch a pressure point you will touch only with the pads of your fingers or the balls of your thumbs. There is no hard and fast rule.
Use whichever finger is most comfortable for you.

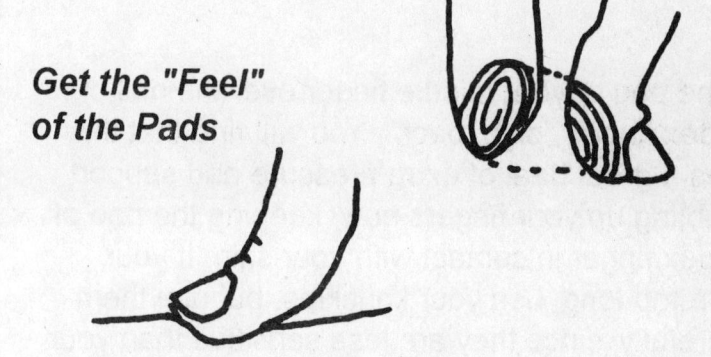

**Get the "Feel"
of the Pads**

The pads of your fingers are those areas that contact the paper when you are being fingerprinted. Practice now by rolling your fingers, one at a time, thumbs included, over a piece of paper or over your skin, getting the "feel" of the pads of your fingers.

If your index fingers are weak, or you need extra pressure for some of the points, double up by crossing your fingers.

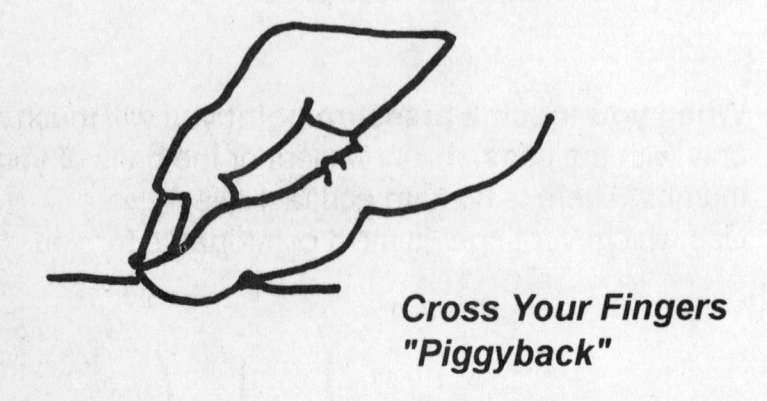

Cross Your Fingers "Piggyback"

Place the pad of your middle finger over the nail of your index finger, "piggyback". You will find that this provides a great deal of extra pressure and support. Try doubling up your fingers now, keeping the pad of your index finger in contact with your skin. If your nails are too long, use your knuckles, but use them very carefully, since they are less sensitive than your fingertips.

When you press, think of your fingers as extensions of your arms, your arms as extensions of your body. As you press, press with your entire body. This does not mean to press hard, but rather with substance, from the center or the core of your body. Practice pressing now.

3. WHERE TO TOUCH

The pressure points are like little magic buttons that are easily found. They feel like little cups, indentations, or notches under the skin.

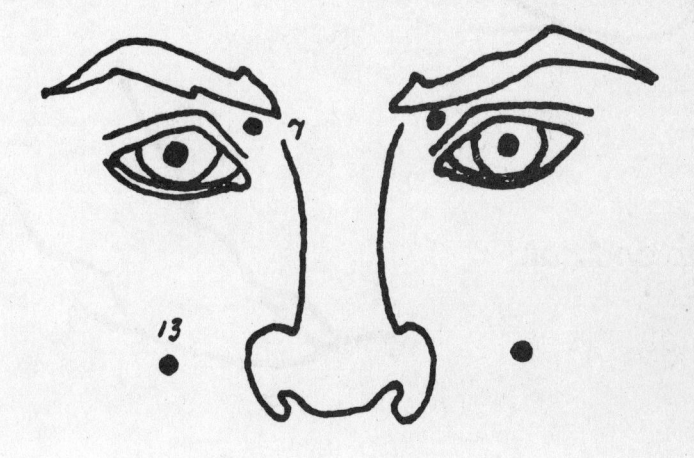

Right now, locate Point 7 found at the top of your eye socket near your nose, just under the eyebrow. Your thumb works best in this large notch. Press carefully. Avoid touching your eyes. Now locate point 13, a cuplike depression located directly below the center of your eye on a line that is about even with the flare of your nostrils.
Each pressure point has an area in which your finger fits comfortably.

Your Basic Technique

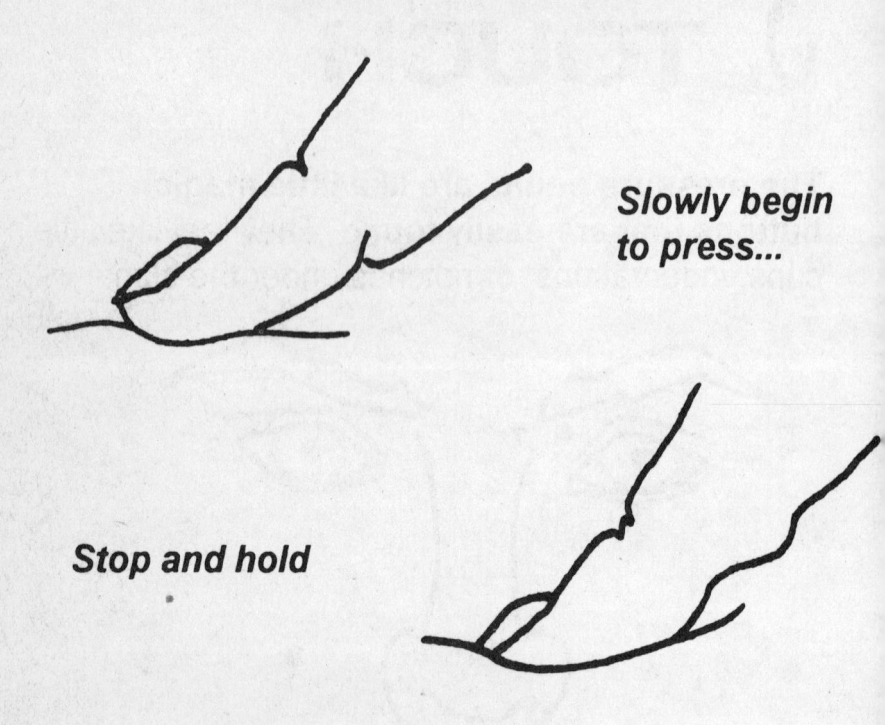

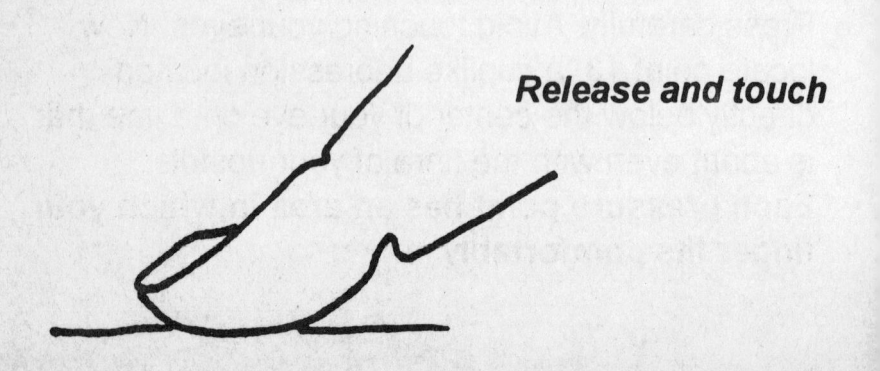

Slowly begin to press...

Stop and hold

Release and touch

4. HOW TO PRESS

The acupressure system is bilateral, so we will be stimulating identical points, simultaneously, on either side of the body. Refer again to Point 13. We will practice our technique here.

To begin, just barely contact the area with the pads of your fingers.

A word of caution: Do not touch any point that is irritated, sunburned, abraded or has an eruption on it. Avoid the area until it has healed.

If Point 13 is clear, **slowly begin to press**, gradually increasing the pressure. Do not rush, and **stay on the pads** of your fingers. (There should be no residual evidence of fingernails.)

Continue to press, proceeding carefully and smoothly. As you gradually approach the juncture between the pleasure of the pressure and the feeling of pain, **STOP! You are now at maximum pressure. Do not go beyond this pressure.**

You do not want to give yourself pain.
You will not get younger any faster.
You will only have a face that reflects pain.

Now, without releasing the pressure,
**hold this maximum pressure for 7 seconds.
Count 1-2-3-4-5-6-7.**

Note: If we were stimulating points on the neck, the pressure would be held for only 3 seconds. But since we are massaging Point 13, a facial point, we hold for 7 seconds.

Now, gradually release the pressure until the pads of your fingers are just very **lightly touching** your skin. Allow them to **rest there for 5 seconds. Count 1-2-3-4-5.**

This is your basic technique.

Practice it again. Ready? Lightly contact the skin. Slowly and smoothly begin to press. When you have reached maximum pressure, which is at the point where the pleasure of the pressure is about to turn to pain, **STOP!**
Hold this pressure for 7 seconds, 1-2-3-4-5-6-7. Now gradually and smoothly release the pressure. *Do not release too quickly.*

When your fingers are again lightly touching the surface of your skin, allow them to rest there for an additional 5 seconds. Count 1-2-3-4-5.
Each point will be stimulated in this manner.

Now run through the entire sequence with repeats. There are 3 repetitions in all. Ready?

Lightly contact .... gradually **Press**....
Hold -2-3-4-5-6-7 .... and **Touch -2-3-4-5**.
The second time, **Press** .... **Hold -2-3-4-5-6-7** ....
Release .... and **Touch -2-3-4-5**. *The third and last time,* **Press** ....**Hold -2-3-4-5-6-7**.... **Release** .... and **Touch -2-3-4-5**. Have you got it?

As you press a point, the pad of your finger must grip the muscle under the skin at all times. **Never rub your finger over your skin and never give yourself pain.**
Remember, from the time your finger touches a pressure point, it remains in contact with your skin until the sequence is completed.

Practice until you are comfortable with the technique. It is important to know how to touch and press. Once you have learned this, basically all that remains is to become familiar with the specific points.

THE TECHNIQUE IN BRIEF

A. When you begin, very gently contact the proper point, just touching the area with your finger pad or ball of your thumb.

B. Begin to press slowly. Gradually increase the pressure. Do not rush. Proceed carefully, smoothly. As you gradually approach the juncture between the pleasure of the pressure and the feeling of pain, Stop!

C. Without releasing the force, hold this maximum pressure for 7 seconds. *Note: Points on the neck are held for only 3 seconds.*

D. Now very gradually release the pressure until the pad is just resting on the skin. Allow it to rest there for 5 seconds

E. Repeat steps B, C, D. The sequence includes 3 repeats in all before moving to another point.

5. BEGINNING THE RITUAL

The entire program includes stimulation of the back of the neck and scalp, the facial points and the bonus, or body, points. Of these, the facial points are required for the actual face lift. The back of the neck and scalp massage is not required, but with it you will get the best results. The bonus, or body points, are very helpful and have been used traditionally to treat and maintain the skin in the Orient. It is suggested that you run through the entire program at least once, so that you can better comprehend the value of the individual segments.

Whenever you begin your ritual, always rub your hands together briskly 50 times to warm and energize them. This energy will be transferred from your hands to the pressure points.

Your attitude is always relaxed.
Your breathing deep and easy.

If possible, **try to coordinate your exhale when pressing and holding at maximum pressure**, particularly if the point being pressed is sensitive.

As you massage you will find yourself yawning. This is good. This is very good. It means that you are releasing pent up energy, eliminating congestion from the meridians, and reestablishing a balanced flow of current in your body.

Progressing through the program, you will become, simultaneously, rested, stimulated and rejuvenated.

6. NECK AND SCALP

THE BACK OF THE NECK AND SCALP MASSAGE

A luxury of ultimate relaxation,
The Back of the Neck and Scalp Massage stimulates necessary circulation to the scalp, neck and face, while removing, pressure, tension and congestion from the areas. There is nothing quite like the overall sense of balance and lightness it offers.

Before we locate the points, *remember to:*

1. Briskly rub your hands together 50 times to warm and energize them.

2. Relax and breathe deeply.

3. Try to exhale when pressing and holding at maximum pressure.

4. Hold maximum pressure for only 3 seconds on the neck area.

5. Repeat the sequence 3 times on each point, your fingers contacting the point throughout the sequence.

6. Avoid any area that is irritated.

The sequence, with repeats, is as follows:

Lightly Contact the point ....
slowly **Press** ....
Hold -2-3 ...
gradually **Release** ....
and **Touch -2-3-4-5** .

The second time,
Press ....
Hold -2-3 ....
Release ....
Touch -2-3-4-5.

The third and last time,
Press ....
Hold -2-3 ....
Release ....
and **Touch -2-3-4-5**.

Back of the Head and Neck Points

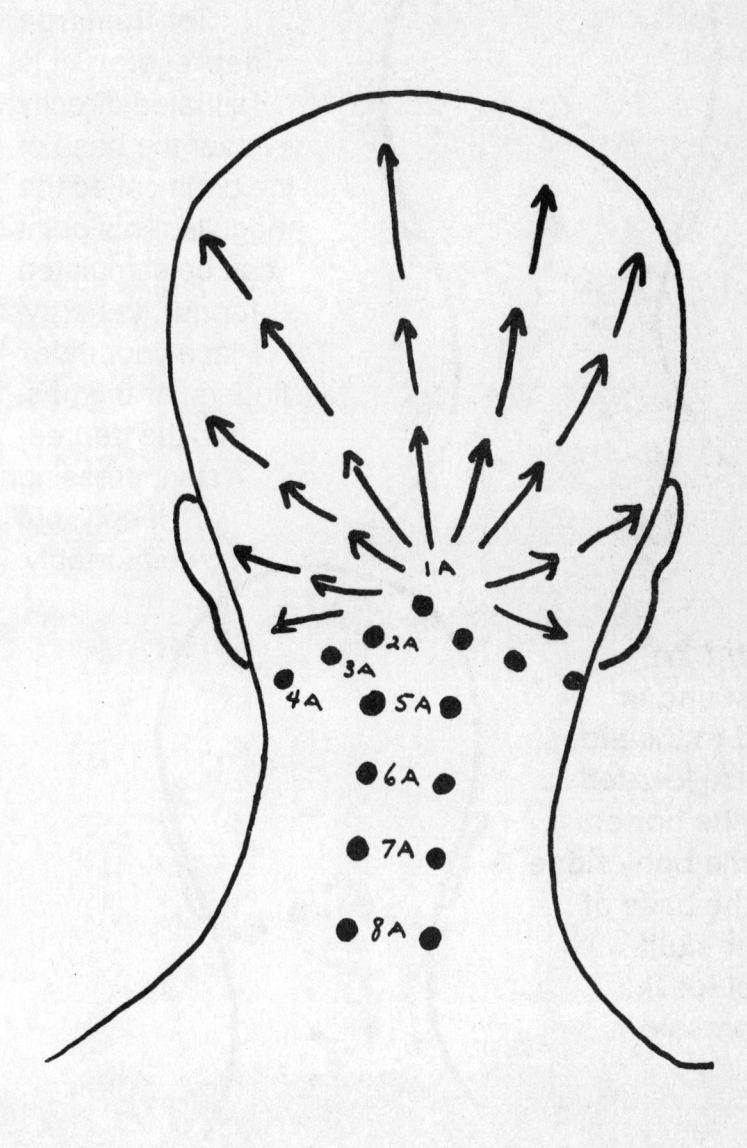

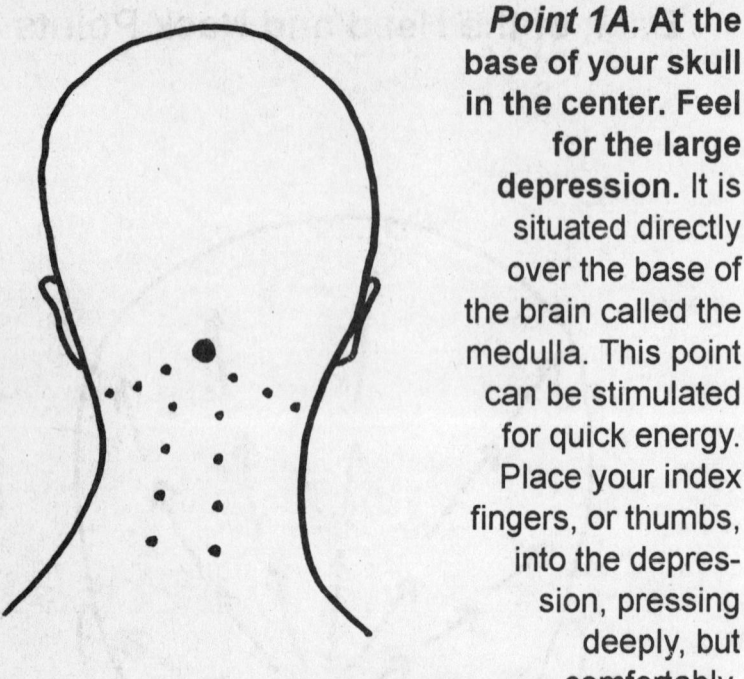

Point 1A. At the base of your skull in the center. Feel for the large depression. It is situated directly over the base of the brain called the medulla. This point can be stimulated for quick energy. Place your index fingers, or thumbs, into the depression, pressing deeply, but comfortably.

Point 2A. Just under and to the sides of 1A, located on the bottom of the bony ridge at the base of your skull. Feel for the depression.

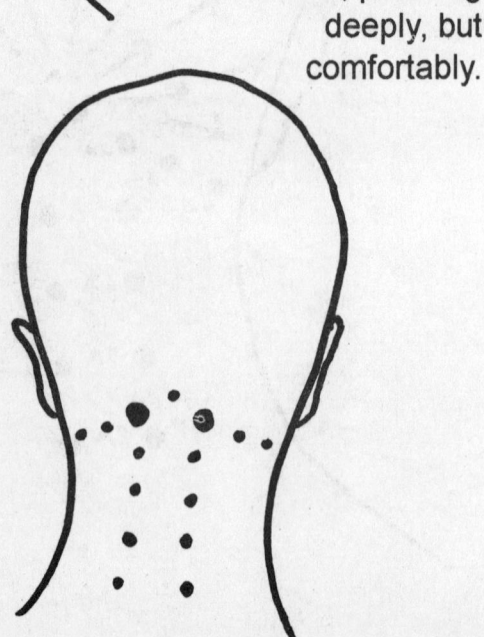

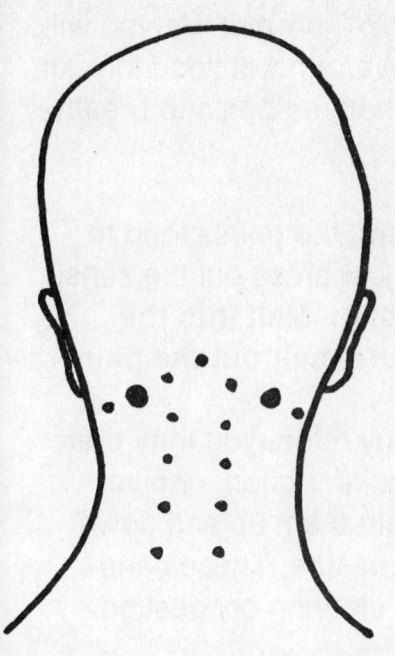

Point 3A. It is the cup or depression next to Point 2A on the bony ridge at the base of your skull, as you move toward your ears.

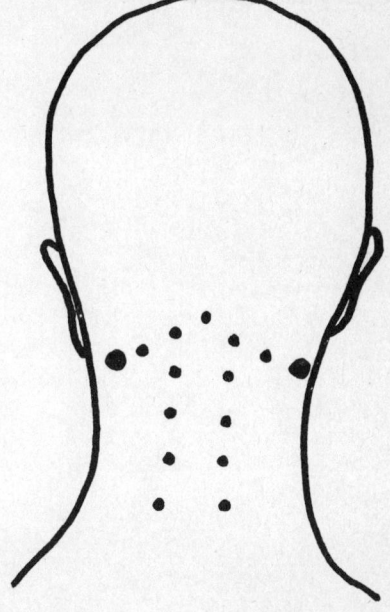

Point 4A. The cup or depression next to 3A on the bony ridge that is closest to the ears. The thumbs work very well here.

As you massage over Points 2A, 3A and 4A, you will feel your head grow lighter. Warmth will flood through your head, and you will find that you begin to breathe very deeply.

As you move closer to the ears, the points tend to become more sensitive. So, just press out the sensitivity. **Gently press out the pain. Melt into the pressure and let the pressure melt out the pain.**

When working across the bony ridge, you may prefer to move your fingers in a circular motion, or pivot them back and forth, or pulsate them up and down when you are at maximum pressure. These variations can be very effective in clearing congestion from the pressure points.

MAXIMUM PRESSURE OPTIONS

During the 3 or 7 seconds maximum pressure, you can opt for any of the four manipulations.

1. **Direct pressure** involves no movement, only direct pressure. This is what we have been using.

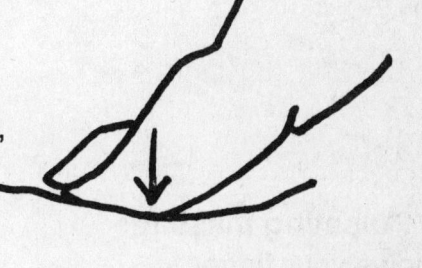

2. **Finger pivoting** employs direct pressure while slowly pivoting the pad of your finger or thumb. Your finger moves back and forth *as much as your skin will allow.* ***Do not stretch your skin!***

3. **Circular motion massage** involves direct pressure, using full, *but very tiny,* rotations of your finger, either clockwise or counterclockwise.

4. **Pulsating massage** allows your finger to pulsate up and down with barely a change from maximum pressure.

These options are exactly that, options. Direct pressure is the simplest and is very effective, but if your want to be more creative, or feel certain points are better stimulated by either pivoting, circular motion or pulsating massage, the choices are yours.

PRACTICING THE OPTIONS

Return now to Point 2A and try *finger pivoting* at maximum pressure. Ready? Press .... **Pivot -2-3** ....
Release .... and Touch -2-3-4-5.
Second time, Press .... **Pivot -2-3** ....
Release .... Touch -2-3-4-5.
Third and last time, Press .... **Pivot -2-3** ....
Release .... and Touch -2-3-4-5.

Now try *circular motion massage* on Point 3A. Ready? Press ... **Circle (outward) -2-3** ....
Release .... Touch -2-3-4-5.
Again, Press .... **Circle -2-3** ....
Release .... Touch -2-3-4-5.
Last time, Press .... **Circle -2-3** ....
Release .... and Touch -2-3-4-5.

Pulse over Point 4A. Ready? Press .... **Pulse -2-3** ....
Release .... Touch -2-3-4-5.
Second time, Press .... Pulse -2-3 ....
Release .... and Touch -2-3-4-5.
Third and last time, Press .... **Pulse -2-3** ....
Release .... and Touch -2-3-4-5.

When you finish, shake out your hands and relax your arms. Breathe deeply.

The options may be used on the facial and body points as well.

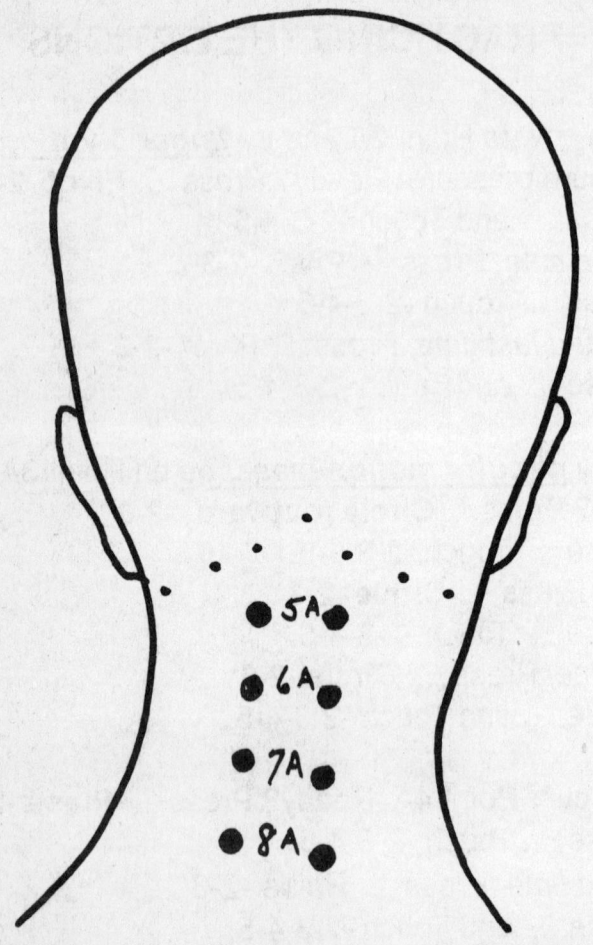

Points 5A - 8A. **Located on the back of the neck on either side of the cervical vertebrae.**

Your technique will be a little different here.

Using your thumbs (or index fingers supported by your middle fingers "piggyback"), press down on each point, while simultaneously pressing your fingers in toward each other. Try it once.

Neck and Scalp Massage

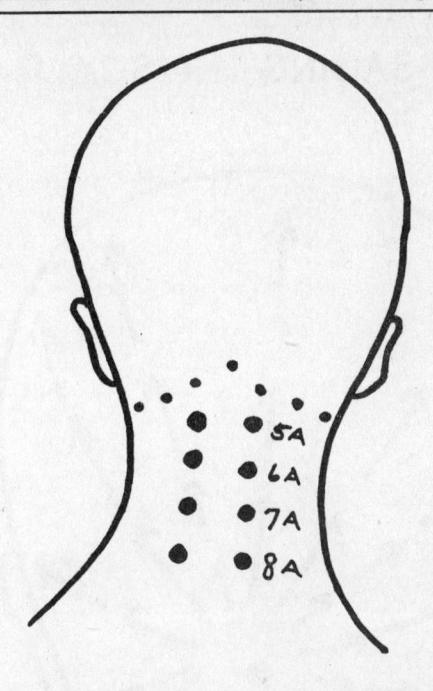

Find **Point 5A**. It is located just below the bony ridge in the soft neck area on either side of the back bone. Now press into your neck, while you also press toward your backbone. Gradually release. Try it again. Press down and in toward your other finger. Have you got it? Stimulate Point 5A two more times. Then, move on to **Points 6A, 7A and 8A**, Each point is stimulated 3 times. Maximum pressure is held for 3 seconds.

When completed, release all tension from your arms. Shake out your hands. Allow your head to loosely drop to your chest. Breathe deeply. Yawn and melt. Your head should feel light, your neck relaxed and filled with warmth.

MASSAGING THE SCALP

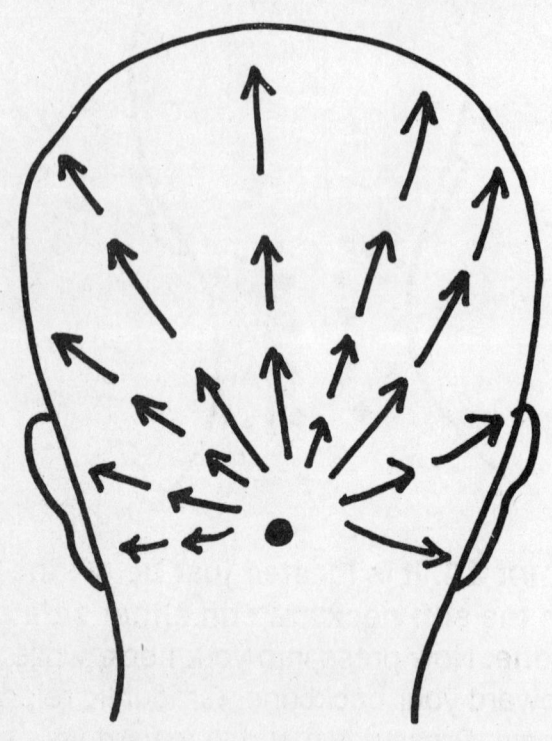

Return to 1A. Place both thumbs into the depression and fan your fingers over your scalp, under your hair. Work over your scalp using the pads of all ten fingers. Massage in little circles, inching little by little toward your hairline. Take several minutes to work over your entire scalp. Allow your pinkies to press deeply into your hairline. Massage behind the ears. Breathe deeply.

Relax your hands, arms and shoulders. Feel all tension dissolve.

THE FACELIFT

42 Facelift Naturally

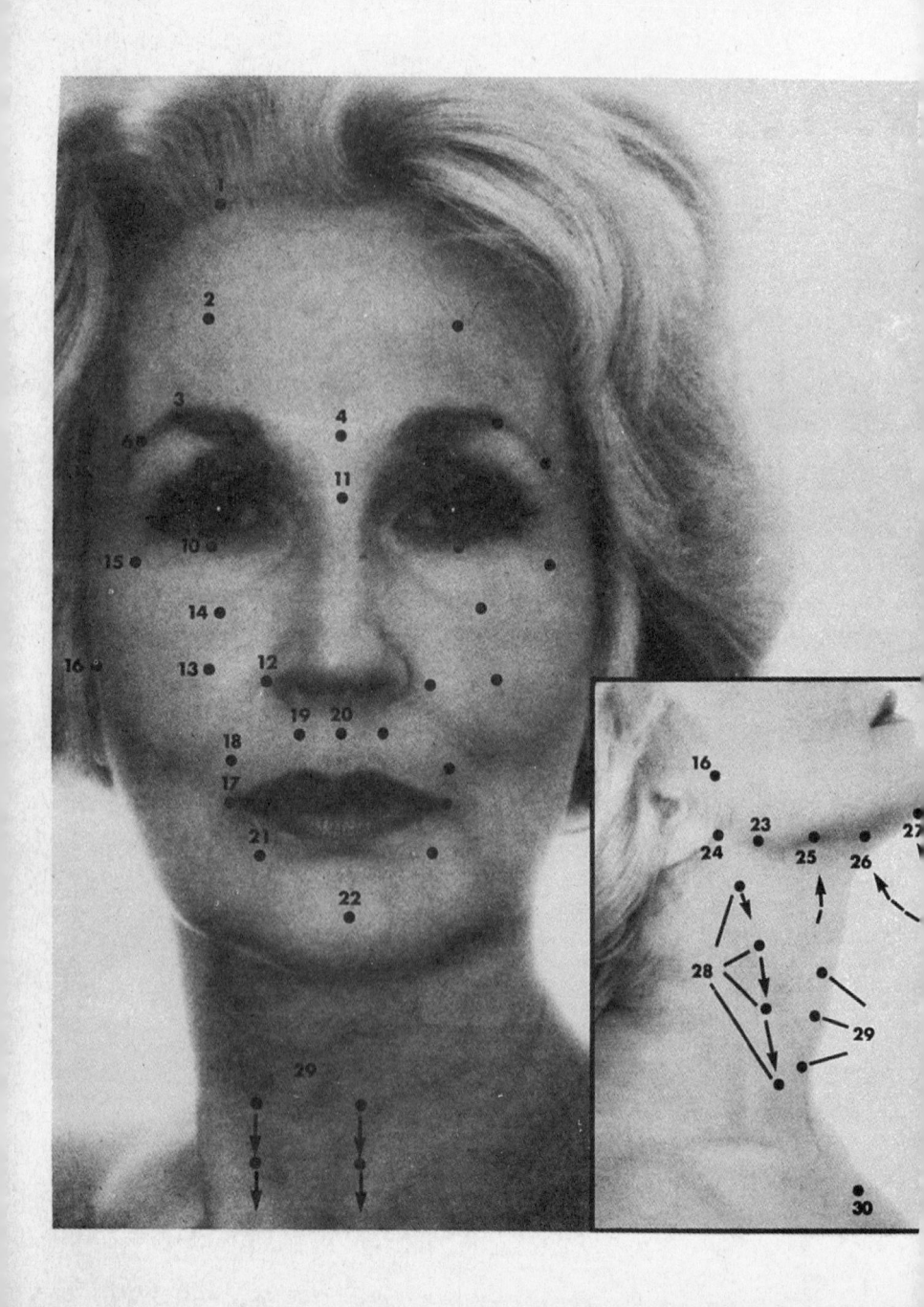

7. THE FACELIFT

Now that we have stimulated luscious circulation in the scalp and neck, we will open the floodgates to the face, which for our purposes begin at the hairline and end at the collar bone.

Note the numerical sequence on your Facial Chart. The format is very logical. Very simply, you begin at the hairline, move down to the eyebrows, circle the eyes and cover the cheek area, which begins at either side of the nostrils, continuing up and around, moving toward the ears. Afterward, points on the lip area will be stimulated, firming first the upper, then the lower lip and the chin.

The final segment is begun behind the ears, continues under the jaw and down the neck, paying particular attention to the thyroid, known as the "seat of beautiful skin". Legend tells us that the ladies of the harem discovered that by massaging the thyroid, they could keep their jealously guarded, exquisitely beautiful skin youthful for a very long time.

From the front of the neck, we move to the back of the neck for a little squeeze. Then knead across the shoulders.... My arms are turning to butter as I type. The anticipation of total relaxation is overwhelming.

For best results when practicing the ritual, follow the numerical sequence. The entire lift includes 30 points. Each point is stimulated for less than one minute, the entire lift taking slightly over 20 minutes.

The program has been divided into areas. If, for some reason, it is not possible to complete the face lift in one session, **you can work in sections**, taking minutes here and there throughout the day.

Please note: When first starting the program, you should for at least one month, practice the entire lift in one sitting daily. Afterwards, one, two or three times a week, depending on your results, condition of your skin and overall health. For faster results, include the Back of the Neck and Head Massage just prior to stimulating the facial points. Also, whenever possible during the day, include the Bonus Body Points. You will find within a short time, like brushing your teeth, the program becomes second nature.

THE FOUR POUND RULE

There are areas on the face in which you may not readily feel pain. In order to avoid injuring your delicate skin, **do not exceed four pounds of pressure on your face.**

An easy way to get the feel of four pounds of pressure is to press your finger on the bathroom scale several times. When you have gotten the "feel", close your eyes and try again. Open your eyes and check the gauge. **Before we locate the facial points, remember to:**

1. Briskly rub your hands together 50 times to warm and energize them.

2. Relax and breathe deeply.

3. Try to exhale when pressing and holding at maximum pressure.

4. Hold maximum pressure for 7 seconds on the facial points unless otherwise directed.

5. Repeat the sequence 3 times on each point, your fingers contacting the point throughout the sequence.

6. Avoid any area that is irritated.

And, to remind you once again of the sequence:

Lightly contact the point ... gently **Press** ....
Hold -2-3-4-5-6-7 .... gradually **Release** ....
and **Touch -2-3-4-5**.

The second time, **Press** ....
Hold -2-3-4-5-6-7 .... **Release** ....
and **Touch -2-3-4-5**.

The third and last time, **Press** ....
Hold -2-3-4-5-6-7 .... **Release** ....
and **Touch -2-3-4-5**.

Note: The Maximum Pressure Options as described in The Back of the Neck and Scalp Massage may be used on the facial points as well.

Also note: If you have opted for circular manipulation, directions for circling have been included on the facial points. The option is yours. You may prefer to work only with direct pressure or combine all variations in one program.

THE FOREHEAD OR BROW AREA

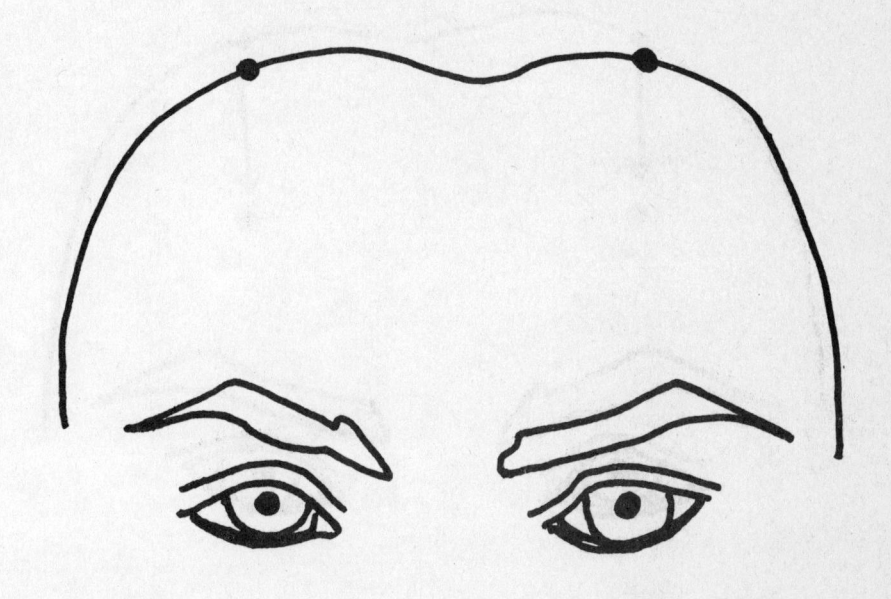

Point 1. Located on your hairline, directly above your eyes, between your scalp and face.
Here you will open up the energy flow from your scalp to your face *(particularly if you have practiced the Back of the Neck and Head Massage first)*. When pressing this point you may feel a response in your abdomen, since you are pressing a point on the Gall Bladder and Liver Meridian. This point is also helpful in relieving headaches. *If circling, circle inward.*

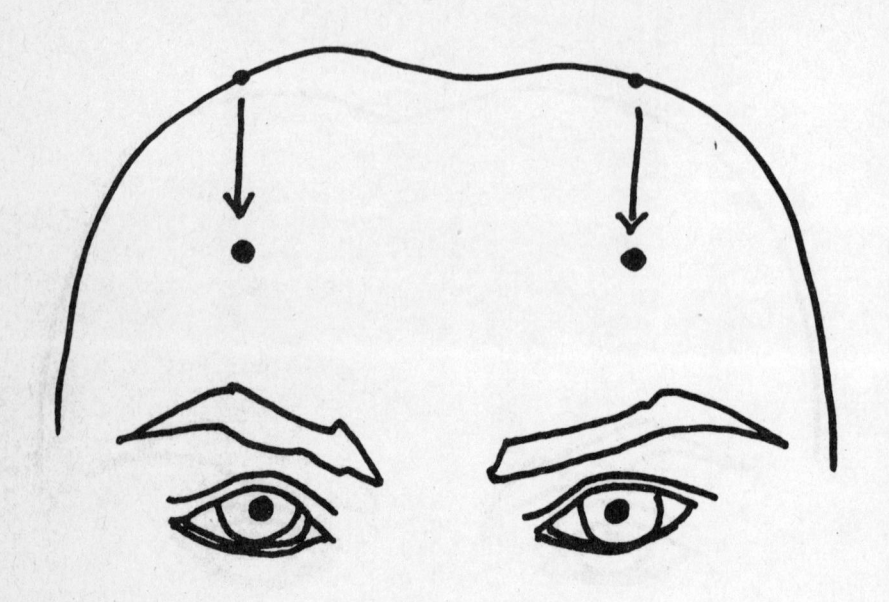

Point 2. **Located just below Point 1, midway between your hairline and your eyebrows.**
As you press and stimulate energy flow, you may start to feel warm throughout your face and the back of your neck. This point is helpful in relieving migraine headaches and insomnia. *If circling, circle inward. Remember the circles are very tiny rotations. Do not, at any time, stretch your skin.*

The Facelift

Point 3. **Located in the center of your eyebrows.**
A tender spot for many, since tension, surprisingly, is often held here. You may find, in fact, that your entire eyebrow area is very sensitive.
If circling, circle inward. Note: Circular motion massage is only one of your options. You may also pulsate, pivot or continue with direct pressure.

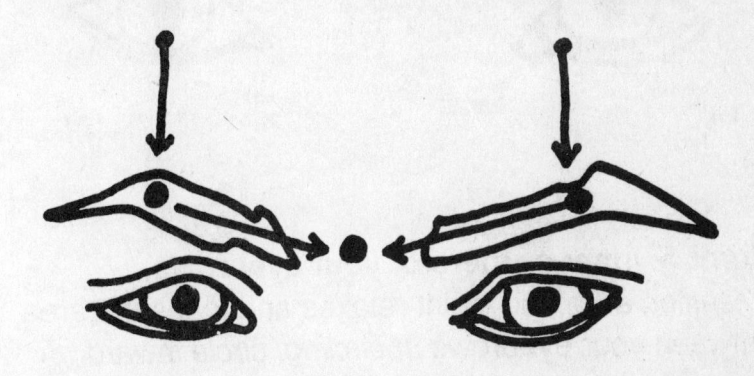

Point 4. **Found between your eyebrows.**
Tap, very lightly, on this point for a minute or two. Feel the entire brow area totally relax. The tapping is very light. Your fingers are relaxed as are your wrists. You can, in fact, barely feel the tapping. But you can feel the energy flowing from the point back into your forehead.

Right about here, I totally relax and go with the flow. **Shake out your hands and relax.**

You have just completed the brow area.

THE EYE AREA

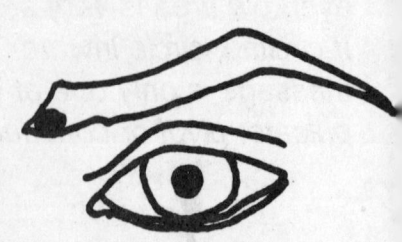

Point 5. Inner corners of your eyebrows.
A tension area, this point relaxes and tones the area between your eyebrows. *If circling, circle inward.*

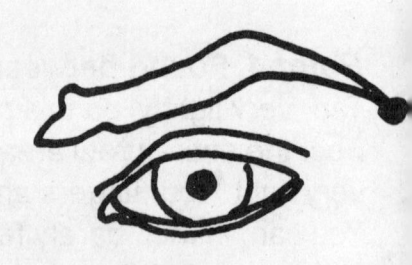

Point 6. On the outer ends of your eyebrows.
Stimulates the muscles above your eyes and temples. It is helpful in smoothing out crowsfeet, also aids in headache relief. *If circling, circle outward.*

Point 7. **At the base of the bridge of your nose.** Feel for the large notches under your eyebrows. The thumb pads work well here. Energy flows from this point around your eyes to the center of your face. This point is helpful in relieving eyestrain, general discomfort of the eyes, sinus problems and headaches. Take care not to touch your eyes when pressing. Pressure is exerted upward.
If circling, circle upward.

Whenever you feel the need for a break, shake out your hands and breathe deeply. Relax any tense muscles. If you are more comfortable and are able to do so, lie down and practice your face lift. I find that soaking in a warm scented bath is a great place to massage, or while lying on a full-body slant board. A major advantage of this lift is that it can be done anywhere, anytime, using 1 finger, if necessary.

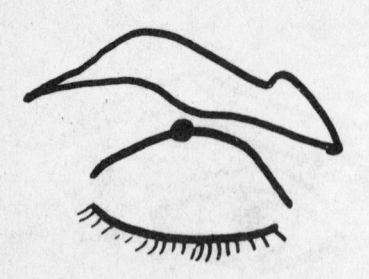

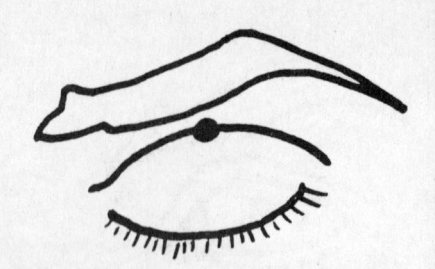

***Point 8.* The small notch in the upper center of your eye socket, on the bone.** This point is helpful for tightening droopy eyelids. It also relieves eyestrain, tension and clears vision. Pressure is exerted upward. Avoid touching your eyes.
If circling, circle upward.

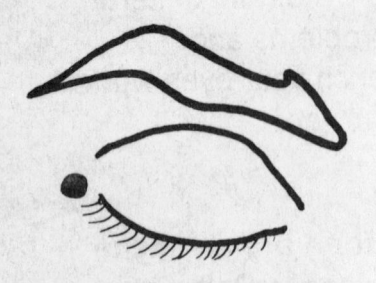

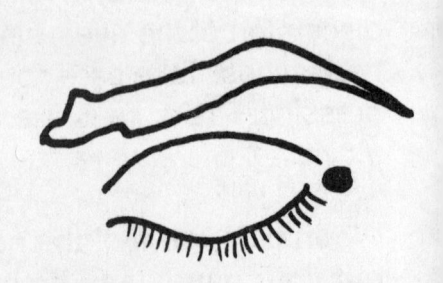

***Point 9.* At the outer corners of your eyes. Feel for the tiny depression in the muscle.** This point is wonderful for circulation around the eyes; it is also of aid in relieving dry eyes and irritation. *If circling, circle outward.*

The Facelift 53

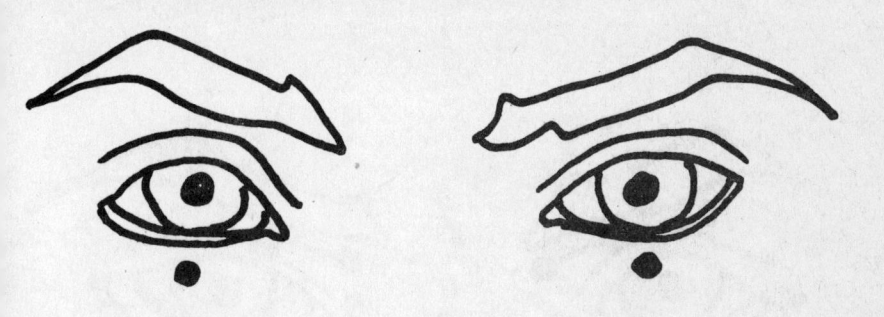

Point 10. In the lower center of your eye sockets, on the ridge of the bone. Feel for a notch.
This point firms bags and the skin under the eyes. It is also helpful in relieving eyestrain and tension. Massage on the ridge of the bone only! Avoid contacting your eyes. *If circling, circle outward.*

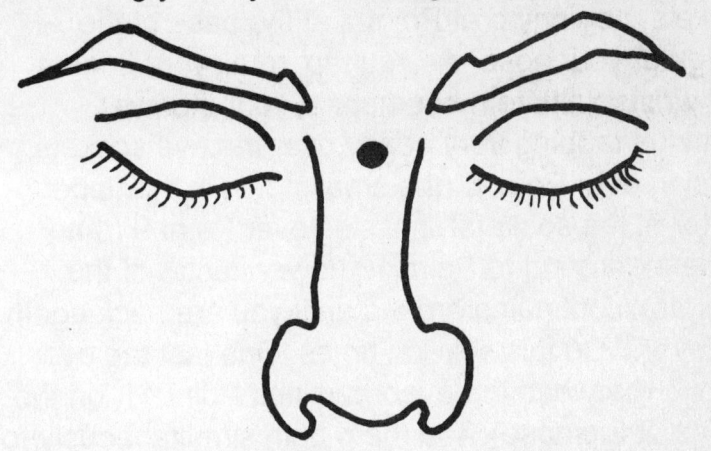

Point 11. On the bridge of your nose. This point firms the area between your eyes.

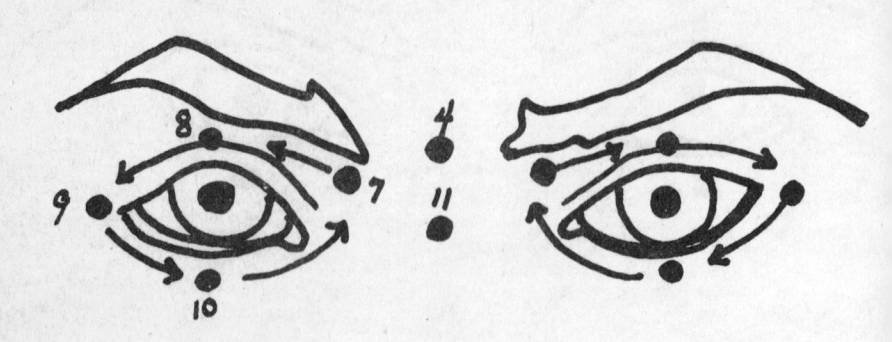

Before you conclude the eye area, lightly tap over the points that you have just stimulated. Using the index fingers of each hand, tap around the entire eye sockets, beginning at Point 7 at the base of the bridge of your nose. As you tap, relax your fingers and wrists. Initiate movement at your elbows. Continue tapping very gently over the eye sockets, passing over Point 8 (the small notch in the upper center of the sockets), passing over Point 9 (outer corners), around to Point 10 (lower center of the sockets), continuing around until you are back again to Point 7. Do this several times. One last tap over Point 4 (between the eyebrows and Point 11, on the bridge of the nose). Tap them both simultaneously for one minute. Then shake out your hands.

**You have just concluded the eye area.
Release tension from your arms and relax.**

The Facelift

FOR YOUR PERSONAL INFORMATION

HOW TO TOUCH YOUR EYES

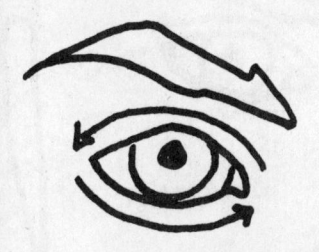

Whenever you touch your eye area, either cleansing, applying creams, oils or makeup, always circle the eye in the direction in which you have been moving in this program-- from the inner corner out when moving over the upper lid, and from the outer corner in on the lower lid.

THE CHEEK AREA

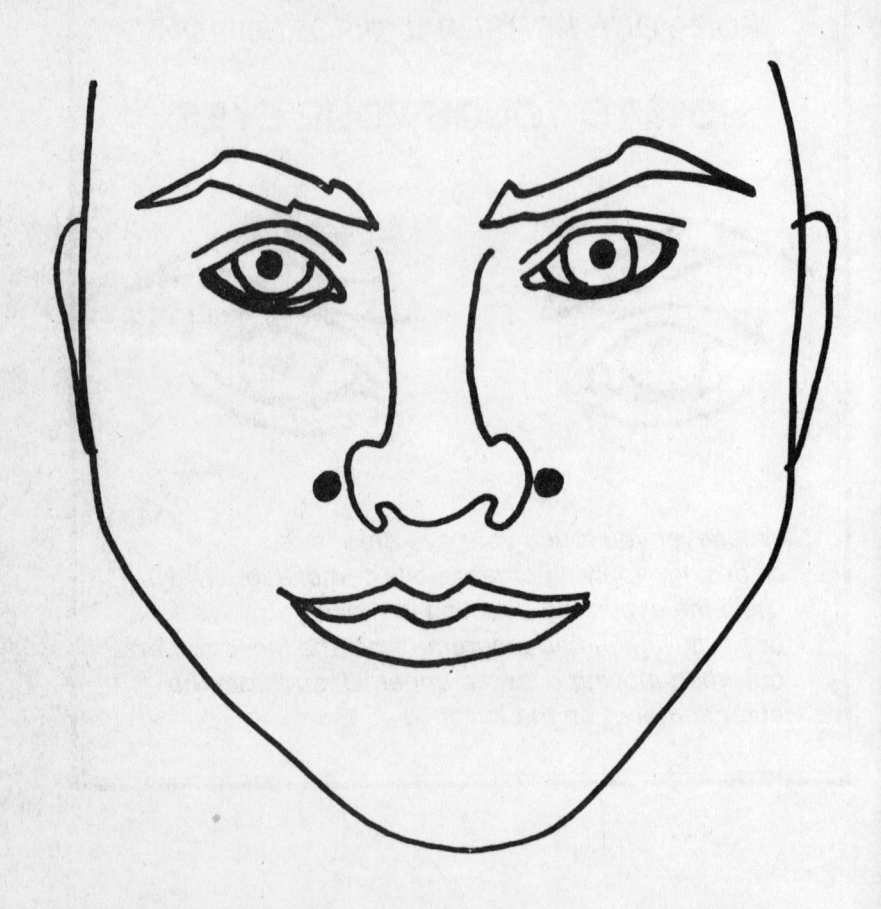

Point 12. On either side of the flare of your nostrils. This is a Large Intestine Point that also works on the nasolabial folds, the lines that appear or are emphasized around or about the mid-thirties. They run from the outside of the nostrils to the corners of the mouth. *If circling, circle outward.*

Point 13. **Directly below the center of your eyes at a line about even with the flare of the nostrils. The depression is located in the front edge of your cheekbones.** This point plumps up flattened tissue in the cheeks restoring the natural contours of your face, brings "roses" to your cheeks and is helpful in sinus relief. *If circling, circle outward.*

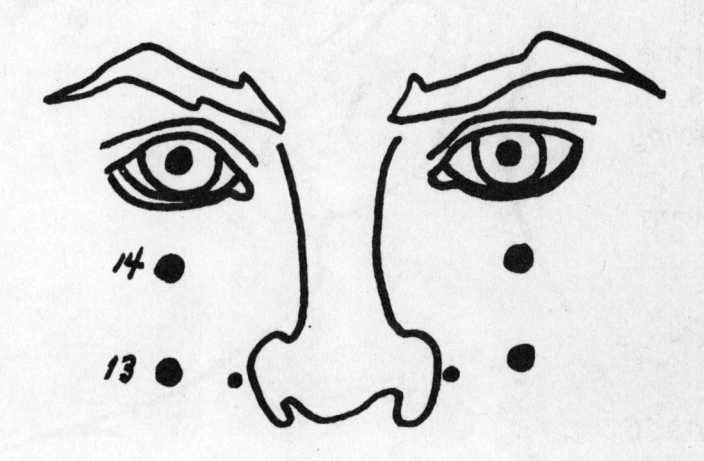

Point 14. **About an inch below your eyes, on a line about even with the midpoint of your nose in a large depression in your upper cheekbones.** The benefits are the same as Point 13. Point 14 is also helpful in filling out small lines on the upper cheeks near the eyes. *If circling, circle outward.*

Point 15. **About one and one-half inches from the corner of your eyes on a line that runs from the corner of your eye to the corner of your jawbone. There is a large depression in the upper cheek, almost at the temple.** This point firms up the cheeks and erases fine lines near the eyes.
If circling, circle outward.

Point 16.
About an inch in front of your ear. Open your mouth slightly to find the depression in the muscle. Pressing this point brings energy to your entire face. It is a great relief for jaw tension.
If circling, circle backward.

The Facelift

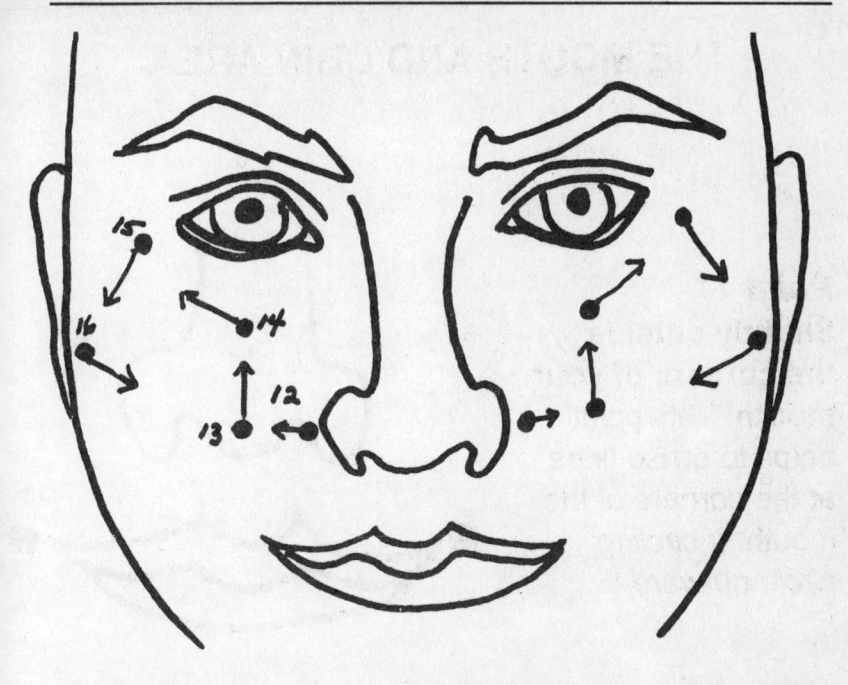

Tap over the points just stimulated, as you did in the eye area. Begin at Point 12 (at either side of your nostrils), continue over Point 13 (below the center of your eyes, even with your nostrils), Point 14 (located an inch below your eyes, even with the midpoint of your nose), Point 15 (an inch and a half from the corner of your eye), Point 16 (an inch in front of the ear) and all the areas in-between. If any area is sensitive, linger there a little longer, stimulating, firming, relaxing and rejuvenating.

When finished, shake out your hands, release the tension in your shoulders, arms and neck.

You have now completed the cheek area.

THE MOUTH AND CHIN AREA

Point 17.
Slightly outside the corners of your mouth. This point helps to erase lines at the corners of the mouth. *If circling, circle outward.*

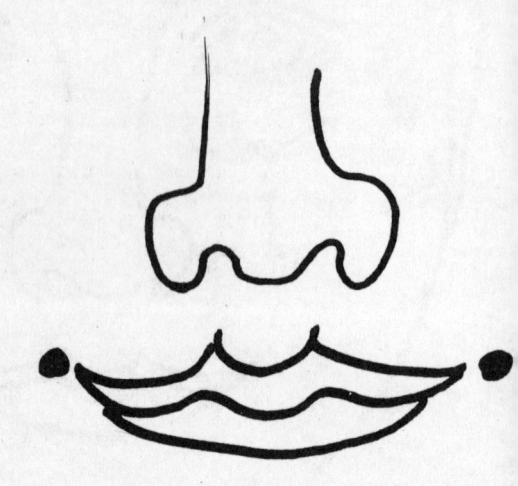

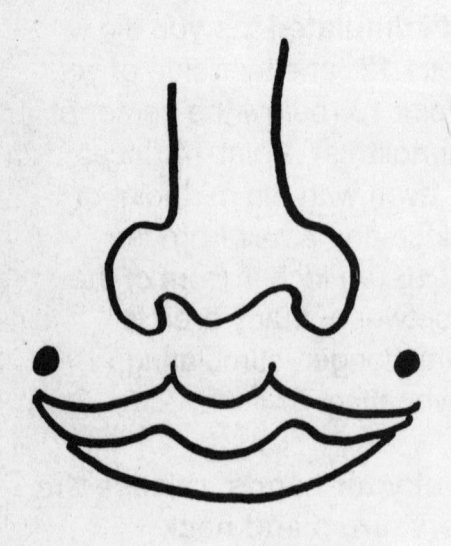

Point 18. One-half inch above the outside corner of your mouth. This point also helps to erase lines at the corners of the mouth. If you have a droopy corner, press here frequently. It will raise it! *If circling, circle outward.*

Point 19.
Under the nostrils, midway to the upper lip. Pressing here helps to erase upper lip lines. *If circling, circle outward.*

Point 20. In the nasolabial cleft, mid-way between the bottom of the nose and the upper lip. Pressing here fills out vertical lines between the nose and the upper lip. It is also an emergency point for nausea, dizziness and fainting.

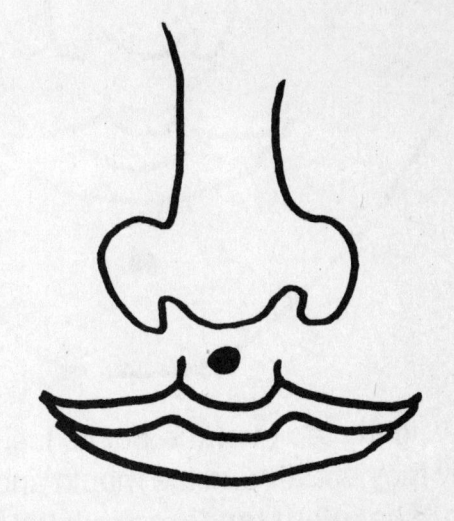

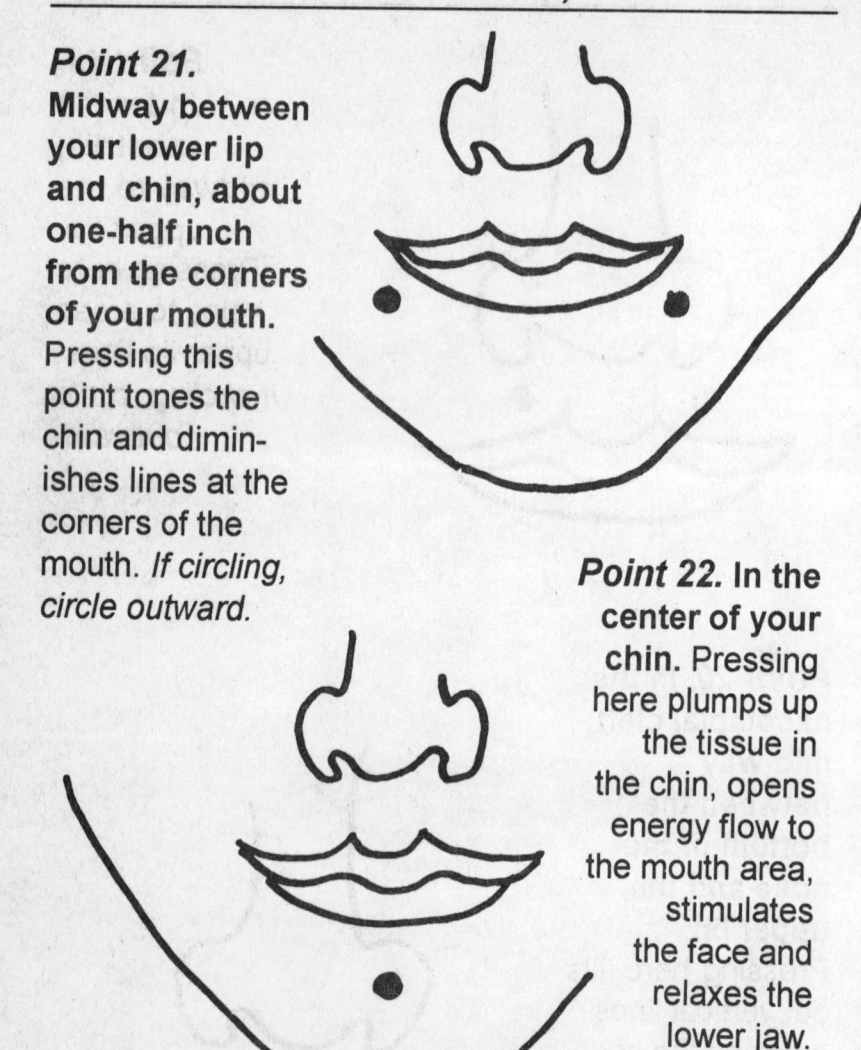

Point 21.
Midway between your lower lip and chin, about one-half inch from the corners of your mouth. Pressing this point tones the chin and diminishes lines at the corners of the mouth. *If circling, circle outward.*

Point 22. In the center of your chin. Pressing here plumps up the tissue in the chin, opens energy flow to the mouth area, stimulates the face and relaxes the lower jaw.

Now lightly tap over the points just stimulated. Essentially they are around the mouth and in the center of the chin. **Shake out tension from your hands and relax. You have just finished the mouth and chin area.**

ADDITIONAL CHANNELS
TO THE FACE AND FIRMING THE NECK

Note: Unless otherwise indicated, hold the following points for 3 seconds at maximum pressure, which means you will **Press** *.... Hold -2-3 ....* **Release** *and* **Touch** *-2-3-4-5 a total of 3 times.*

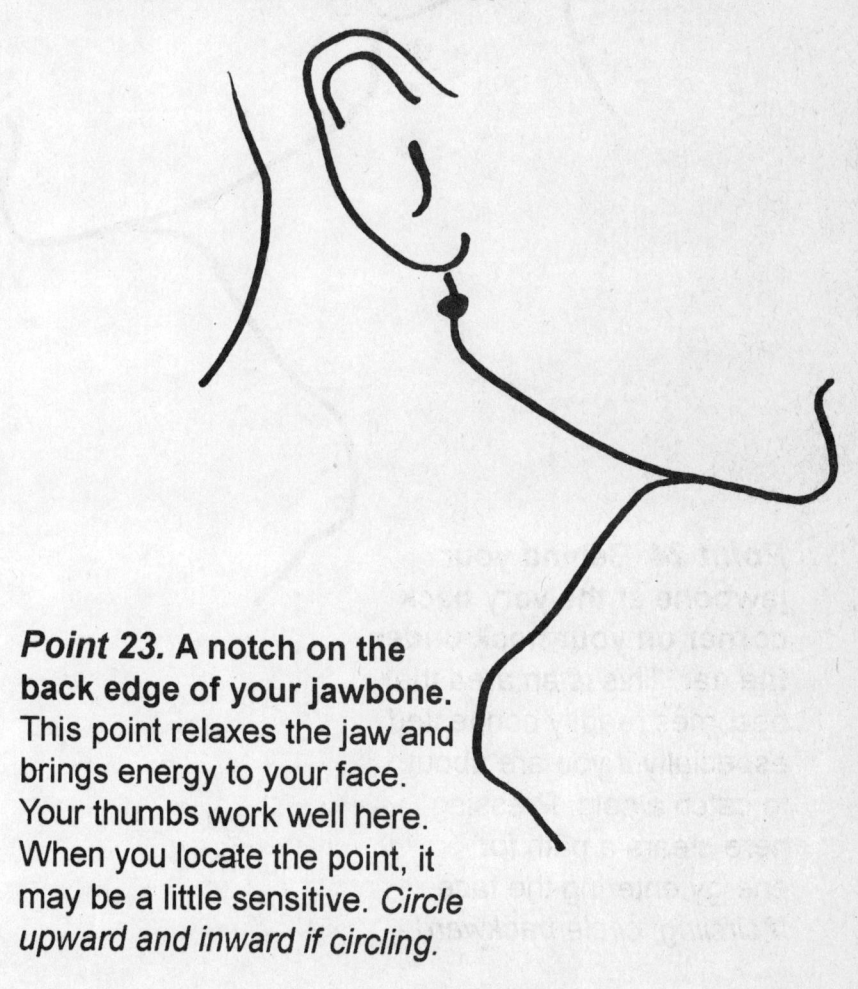

Point 23. **A notch on the back edge of your jawbone.** This point relaxes the jaw and brings energy to your face. Your thumbs work well here. When you locate the point, it may be a little sensitive. *Circle upward and inward if circling.*

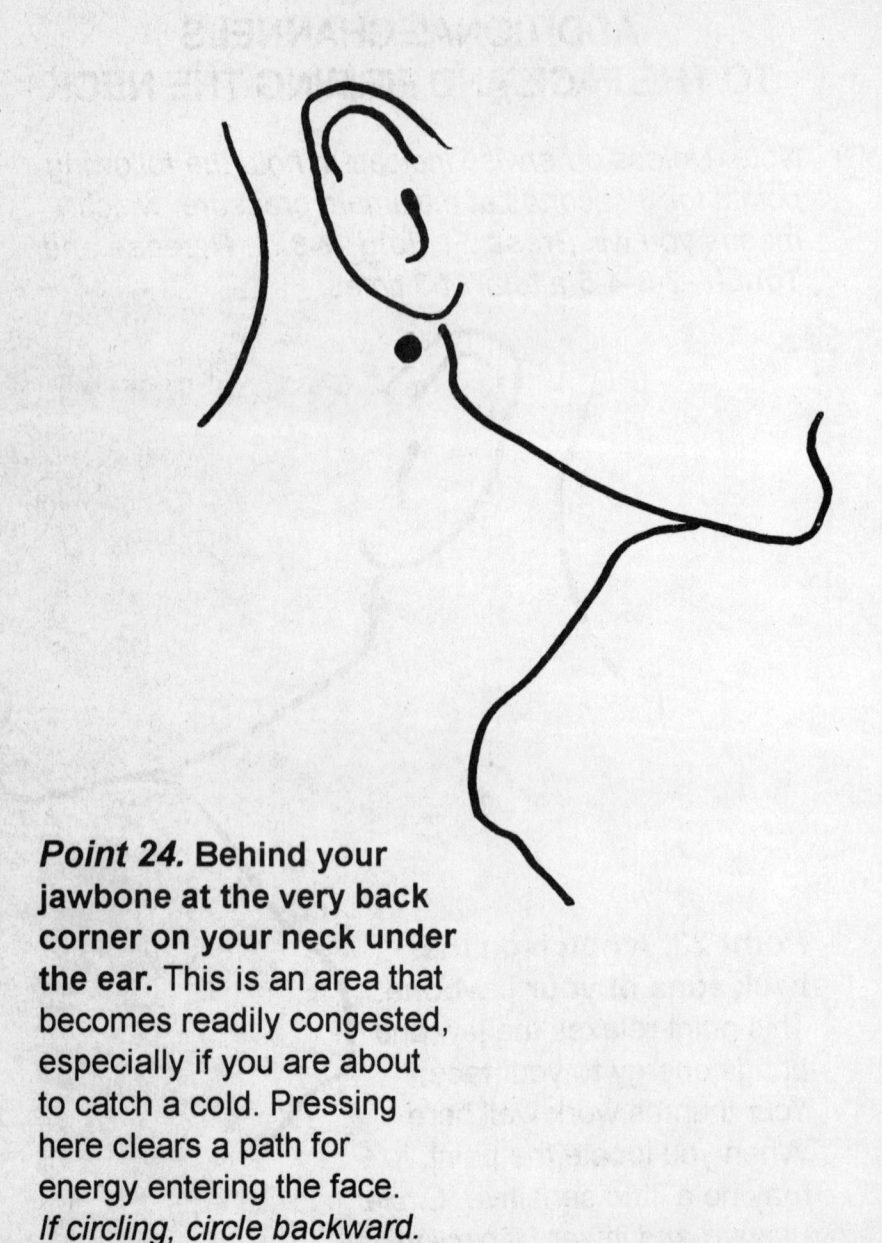

Point 24. Behind your jawbone at the very back corner on your neck under the ear. This is an area that becomes readily congested, especially if you are about to catch a cold. Pressing here clears a path for energy entering the face.
If circling, circle backward.

The Facelift

Point 25. Under the jawbone in a deep depression about 1 inch from the back corner.
Hook your thumbs under the jawbone and massage out the glands behind the bone. This can be a very sensitive area. If when pressing you feel little "bubbles" under your thumbs, massage them out. This is congestion. Massaging here will bring energy to the face and tighten the neck area.
If circling, circle backward and in toward the neck.

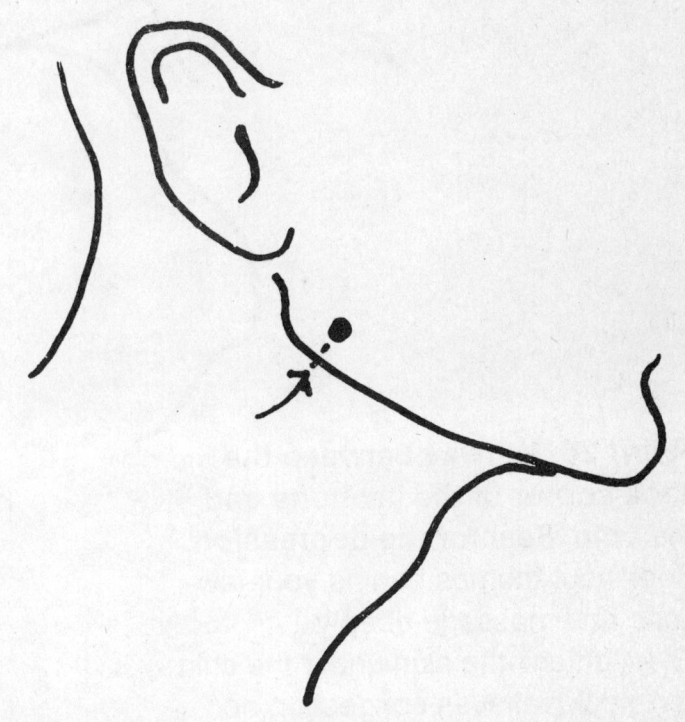

Note: When an area is congested, you may feel stress in your fingers. If this happens, be sure to shake out your hands, or rinse them in cool water.

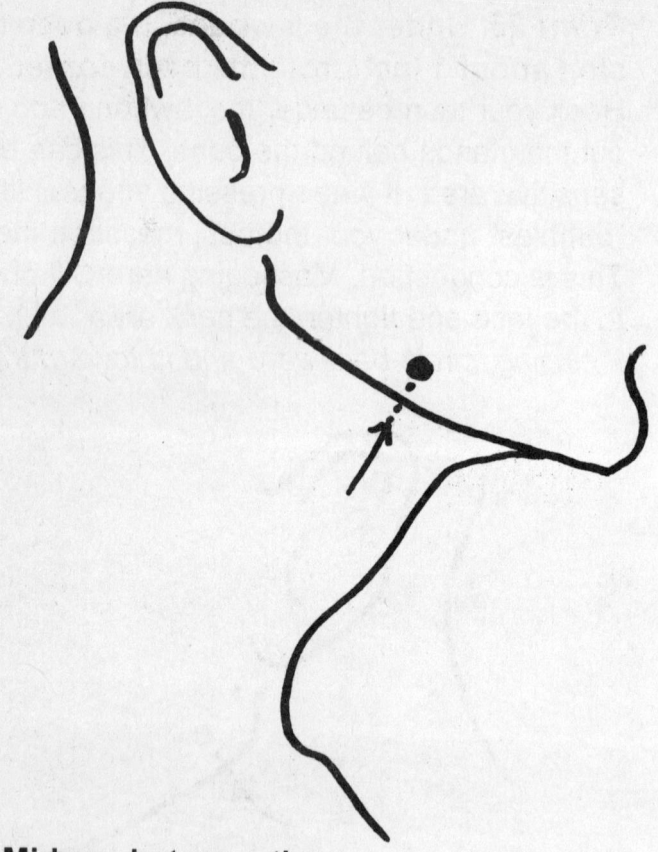

Point 26. Midway between the back corner of the jawbone and the chin. Feel for the depression. Hook your thumbs behind your jawbone and massage deeply.
This tightens the skin under the chin and neck, relieves congestion and increases the energy flow to the face.
If circling, circle forward and into the bone.

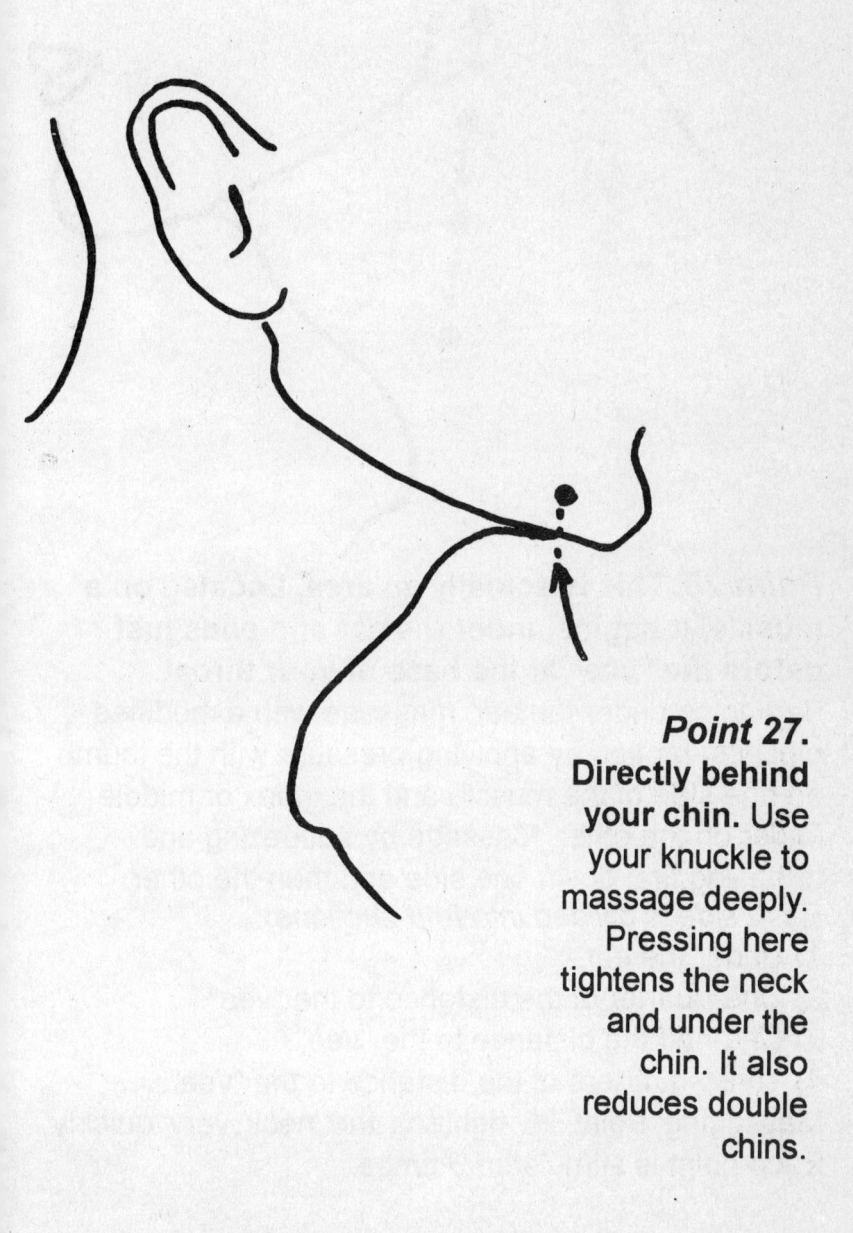

**Point 27.
Directly behind
your chin.** Use
your knuckle to
massage deeply.
Pressing here
tightens the neck
and under the
chin. It also
reduces double
chins.

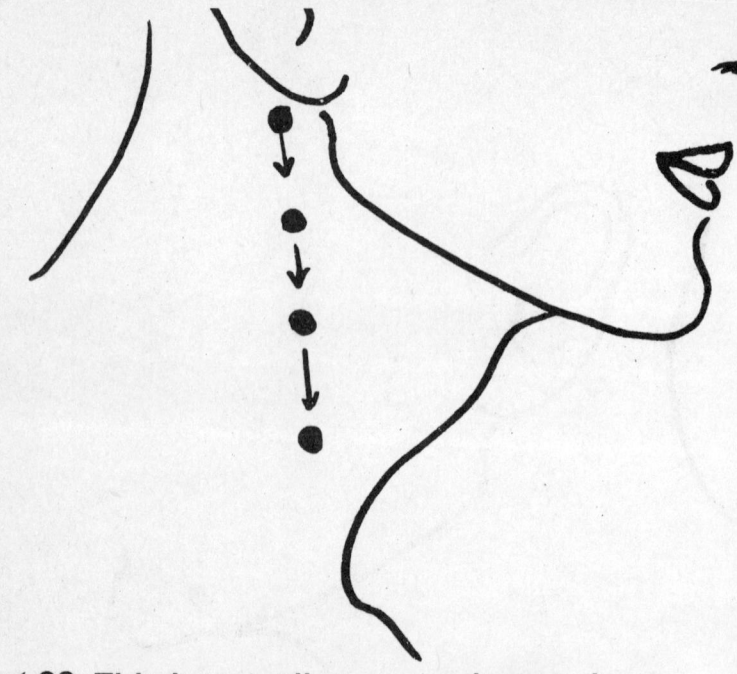

Point 28. **This is actually an area. Located on a muscle, it begins under the ear and ends just before the "vee" at the base of your throat.** Beginning under the ear, massage with a modified pinching motion by applying pressure with the thumb on one side of the muscle and the index or middle finger on the other. Massage by squeezing and releasing first down one side and then the other.
Each side is divided into four sections:
1) Under the ear.
2) One-quarter of the distance to the "vee".
3) One-half the distance to the "vee".
4) Three-quarters of the distance to the "vee".
Massaging Point 28 tightens the neck very quickly. Each point is stimulated 3 times.

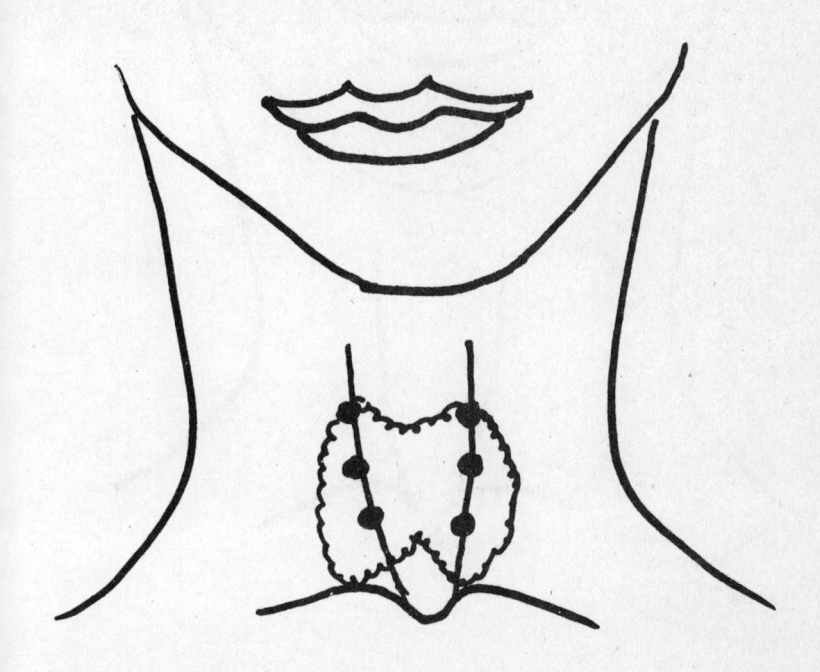

Point 29. About halfway down the neck, over the thyroid gland, on either side of your windpipe. This point can be stimulated in one of two ways:
   1) Using 3 fingers of each hand, vibrate the area or
   2) Using a modified pinching motion, quickly and gently squeeze and release the point.

If squeezing, expect a little cough. Repeat whichever method you select 3 times. *The thyroid is a major factor in body metabolism and weight control.* Stimulating this point increases systemic energy and firms the neck as well.

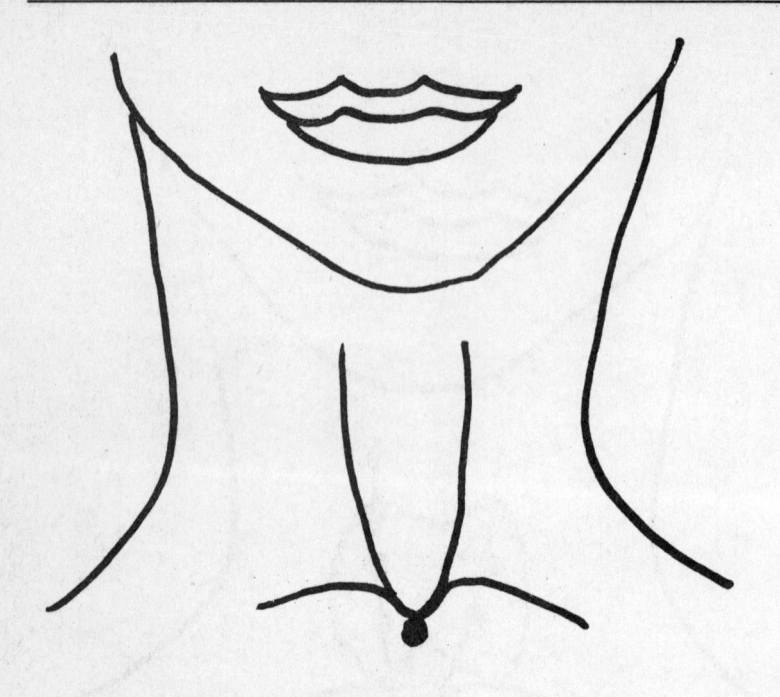

Point 30. **In the notch of the bone at the base or "vee" of your throat.** Energy is directed up into the neck and head from your body through this point. Press on the bone only. This point can relieve hoarseness and colds as well.
Maximum pressure on this point is held for 7 seconds.

Bravo! **You have completed the facial points!**

Be sure to shake out your hands, relax your arms and release all tension.

Now, reach around to the back of your neck and give your neck a little squeeze, first with one hand and then with the other. Knead across your shoulders beginning at the base of your neck. Mmmmm .... doesn't that feel good? Work all the way across your shoulders. **When you have completed this, shake out your hands, your arms, release your neck and head. Breathe deeply and melt.**

Can you feel your face and neck beginning to tighten, your facial tissue plump? I could from the very first massage. You should *at the very least look more relaxed, more radiant, more alive!*

You must repeat your ritual again tomorrow and every day for a month. If you are satisfied with your progress at the end of that time, maintain your lift by massaging two or three times weekly. For some people, once a week may be sufficient. Each day you practice the lift you will see a little more improvement, and each time you lift, the lift will hold a little longer. Results may be seen ordinarily in a week or more, rejuvenation in about a month, depending on your skin condition and overall systemic vitality.

If at the end of a month you want to see more improvement, continue with the daily ritual. Heavy wrinkles will take longer and cosmetic lifts that have sagged will also take more time due to the scarring

and the disruption of the meridians by surgery.
As with the benefits of total body exercise, *Facelift Naturally* bestows its benefits as long as it is practiced. If for some reason you have to stop lifting for several weeks, begin at the beginning, massaging daily. Your lift should return quickly, since your skin has a memory and will respond.

It is highly improbable that you will stop, however, since you can lift practically anywhere, watching TV, talking on the phone, waiting for the bus, sitting at a stoplight. Once you know the points, you can just push your "lift" buttons anytime.

Well, there you have it.
Happy Lifting!

8. THE BONUS POINTS

Traditionally employed in the Orient for the treatment and maintenance of the skin, the following 7 body points can be individually stimulated at any time during the day with excellent results. If time allows, by all means incorporate them into your daily ritual. Pressing these seven points daily is reputed to improve skin tone and texture, while improving body condition

Each point is manipulated as follows:

    Lightly **Contact** the point .... slowly **Press** .... **Hold** -2-3-4-5-6-7 .... gradually **Release** .... and **Touch** -2-3-4-5.

    Again, lightly **Contact** .... slowly **Press** .... **Hold** -2-3-4-5-6-7 .... gradually **Release** .... **Touch** -2-3-4-5.

    Last time, Lightly **Contact** the point .... slowly **Press** .... **Hold** -2-3-4-5-6-7 .... gradually **Release** .... and **Touch** -2-3-4-5.

The Technique

The technique is the same basic technique that we have been using. All bonus points are held for the count of 7.

1. Briskly rub your hands together 50 times to warm and energize them.

2. Relax and breathe deeply.

3. Try to exhale when pressing and holding at maximum pressure particularly when a point is sensitive as several of these can be.

4. Hold maximum pressure for 7 seconds.

5. Repeat the sequence 3 times on each point; your fingers remain in contact with your skin through all 3 repeats.

6. Avoid contact with any area that is irritated.

The Bonus Points

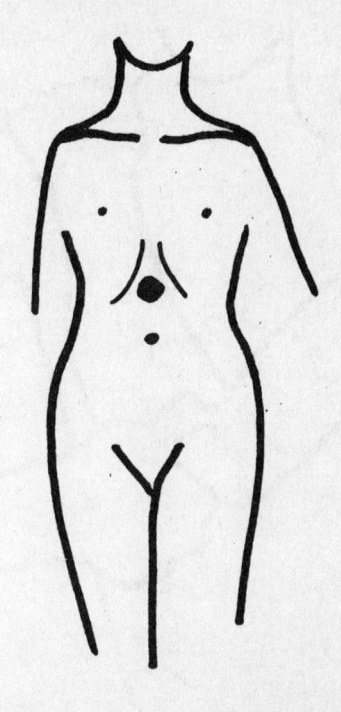

Point 1B. **Located in the pit of your stomach. Use 3 fingers of each hand to press in deeply. Remember to exhale as you press in. Point 1B helps to control the general condition of the internal organs and distributes nourishment.**

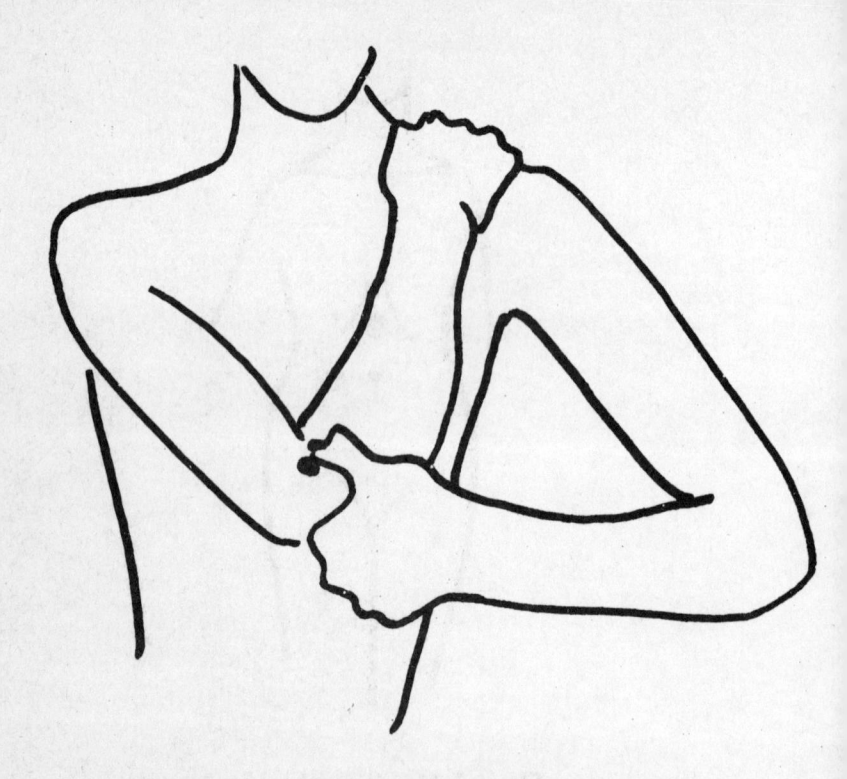

***Point 2B.* To locate, place one hand over your opposite shoulder.** Following the crease of your flexed elbow to the base, you will find a notch just above and against the bone. Press deeply, massaging your right arm with your left hand and vice versa. Pulsing, pivoting or circular motion massage work well here.

The Bonus Points

Point 3B. Located in the web between your thumb and index finger way up into the web where the bones meet. Use a modified pinching motion, pressing deeply.

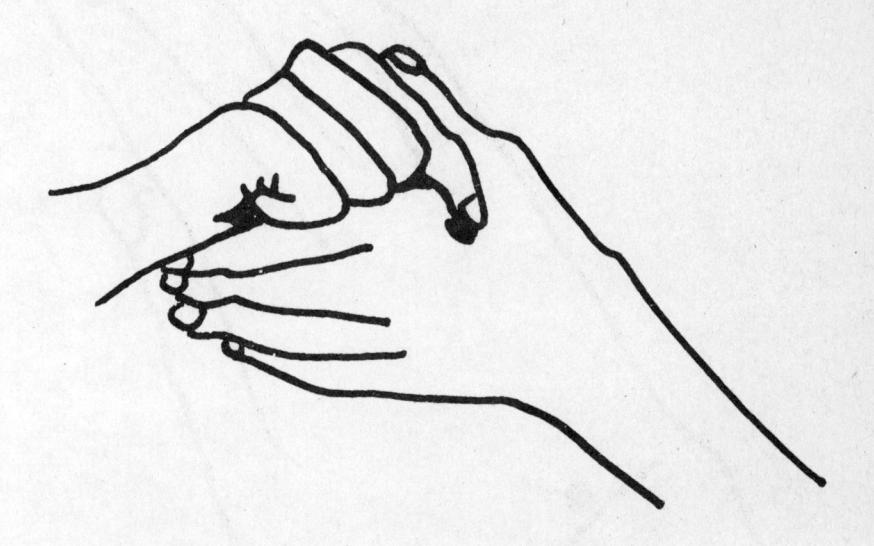

Often very sensitive, this point is a master point for the head and neck and a direct line to the Large Intestine. Pressing here can clear a headache in seconds, especially if it is connected to sluggish digestion. Massage one hand and then the other, by placing the thumb on one side of the point and the index finger on the other. Circular motion works particularly well on this point.

Point 4B. To locate, flex your hand backward to find the wristline.

The point is on the back of your hand in the center, directly below the wristline. Massage both wrists.

The Bonus Points

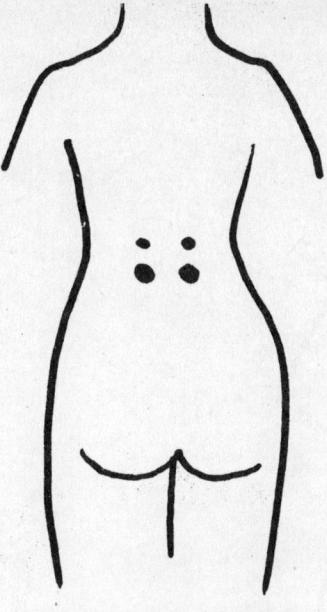

**Point 5B.
Located on either side of your second lumbar vertebra.**

Easily found, the lumbar region of your backbone is located between the lowest pair of ribs and your pelvis. *There are five vertebrae in the lumbar region. Count under the ribs, 1-2 ... and there you are.* Situated directly over the adrenal glands, massaging here will stimulate positive energy flow. Knuckles seem to work best for stimulation.

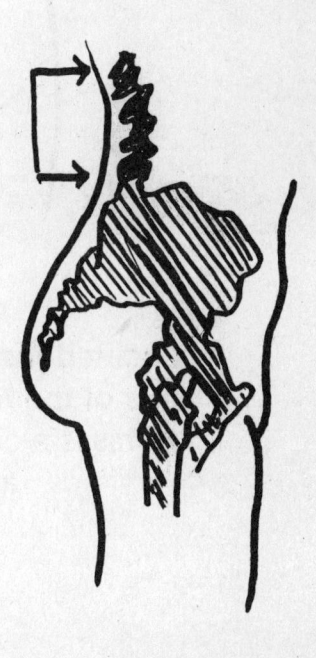

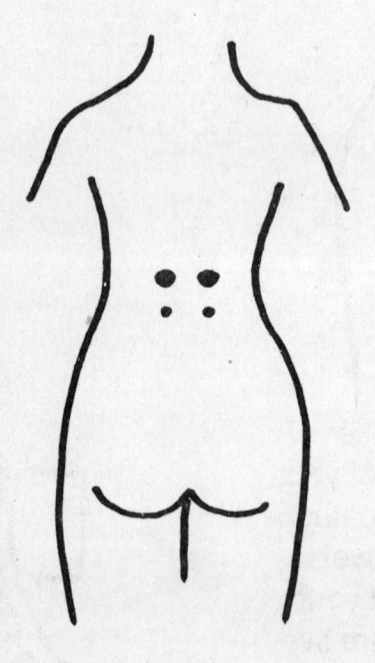

Point 6B.
Located just above 5B on either side of the first lumbar vertebra. This is a control point for food absorption.

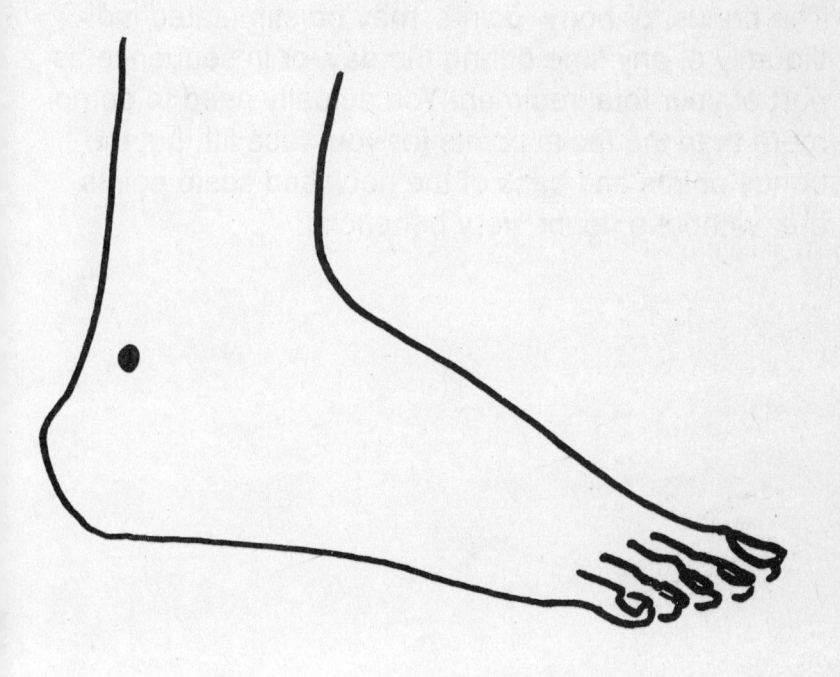

Point 7B. Found on your foot, behind the ankle bone, just above your heel at the Achilles tendon. Use a modified pinching motion with your thumb and index finger. This area is usually very tender. Press as deeply as possible. Massage both feet. *If circling, circle toward the heel.* You are stimulating both the Bladder and Kidney meridian.

Remember to shake out tension from your hands as you work. Breathe deeply and relax, exhaling at maximum pressure.

The bonus, or body points, may be stimulated individually at any time during the day, or in sequence as part of your total regimen. You actually need to do no more than the facial points for your face lift, but the bonus points and back of the neck and scalp points are, without a doubt, very beneficial.

9. MINI-LIFTS FOR PROBLEM AREAS

A Mini-Lift may be used in two ways: It may be used as a supplement to your daily ritual during the first month for areas that require intensive work, or it may be used daily after your initial month, while the full lift is practiced, one, two or three times a week.

The procedure for the Mini-Lifts is the same as for the Facelift. *Remember to:*

1. Briskly rub your hands together 50 times to warm and energize them.

2. Relax and breathe deeply.

3. Try to exhale when pressing and holding at maximum pressure.

4. Hold maximum pressure for 7 seconds, unless stimulating a neck point, where pressure is held for 3 seconds, or unless instructed otherwise.

5. Avoid stimulating any area that is irritated.

6. Massage each point 3 times in sequence, as in the Facelift, unless otherwise indicated.

THE FOREHEAD OR BROW

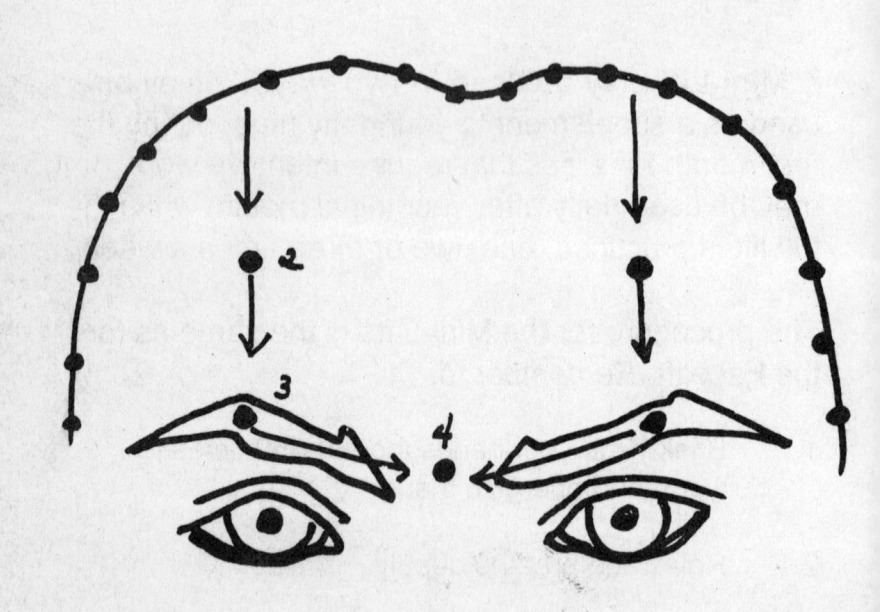

Areas stimulated: *Hairline, Points 2, 3, 4.*

Point 2. Directly above your eyes, midway between your hairline and eyebrows.

Point 3. Center of your eyebrows.

Point 4. Between your eyebrows.

Massage your hairline with the pads of the four fingers of each hand until the area is warm and tingles. Then massage Points 2 and 3 in the regular manner for 7 seconds at maximum pressure. Follow by tapping over Point 4 for 1 minute.

GENERAL EYE LIFT I

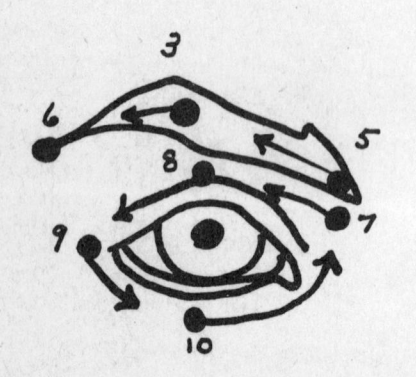

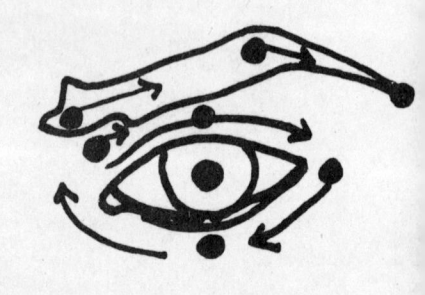

Areas stimulated: *Points 5, 3, 6, 7, 8, 9, 10.*

Point 5. At the inner corners of your eyebrows.

Point 3. Center of your eyebrows.

Point 6. Outer end of your eyebrows.

Point 7. At the base of the bridge of your nose, under your eyebrows.

Point 8. Notch in upper center of your eye socket, on the ridge of the bone.

Point 9. Outer corners of your eyes.

Point 10. Notch on the ridge of the bone in the lower center of your eye socket.

Massage Points 5, 3, 6 - 10 in order as follows: Press to maximum pressure using a slow count of 10, but instead of holding at maximum pressure, immediately begin to release to a slow count of 10. Then, tap over each point, lightly, for another count of 10. Got it? Press for 10, Release for 10, Tap for 10, then move to the next point and repeat the sequence.

GENERAL EYE LIFT II
Back of the Neck and Head Massage

To be used in conjunction with the General Eye Lift I
Maximum pressure is held for 3 seconds.

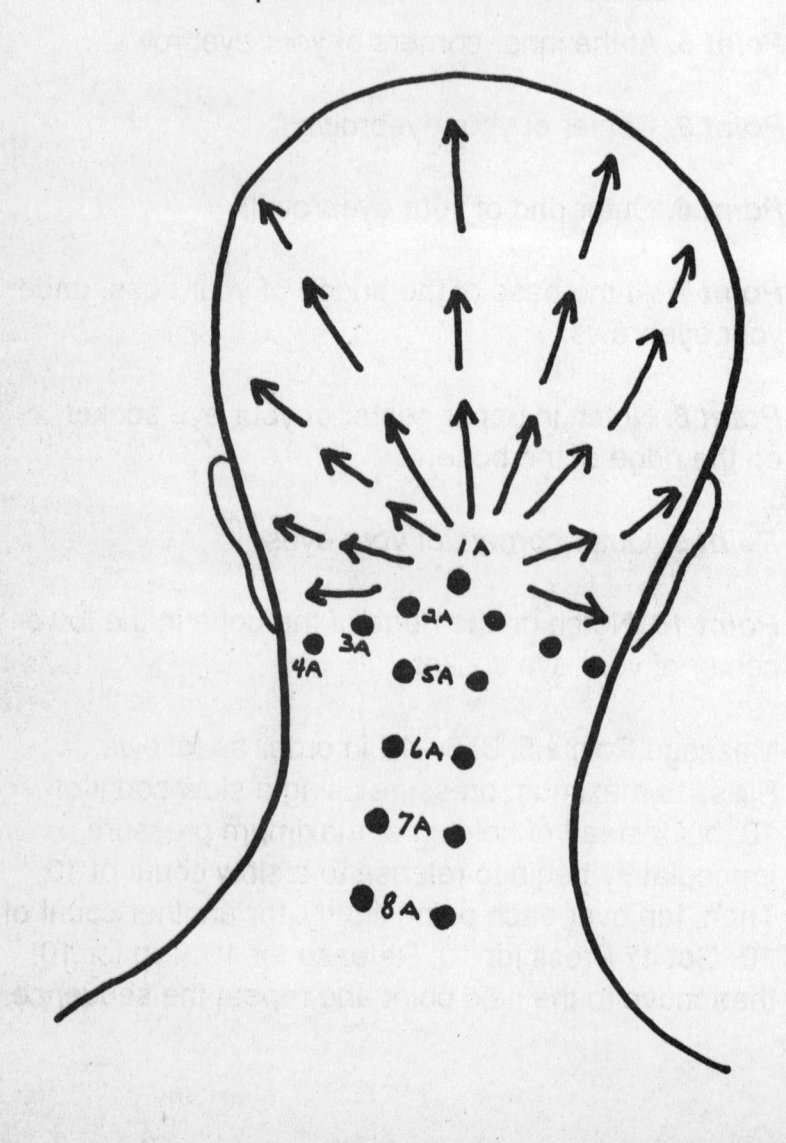

Areas stimulated: *Points 1A - 8A.*

Point 1A. Central depression at the base of your skull.

Points 2A - 4A. Along the bony ridge at the base of your skull.

Points 5A - 8A. On either side of your cervical vertebrae.

Stimulate as in the Back of the Neck and Scalp Massage. To refresh your memory see pages 31 - 34 and pages 38 - 40.

UPPER LID LIFT

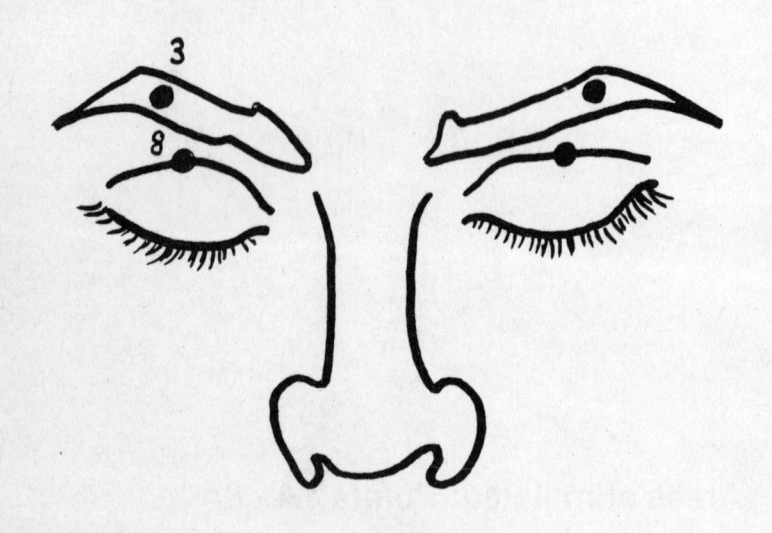

Mini-Lifts for Problem Areas

Areas stimulated: *Points 3, 8.*

Point 3. Center of your Eyebrows.

Point 8. Center notch in your upper eye socket.

Lightly tap for 1 minute and/or press in the regular manner for 7 seconds at maximum pressure.

AREA BETWEEN THE EYES

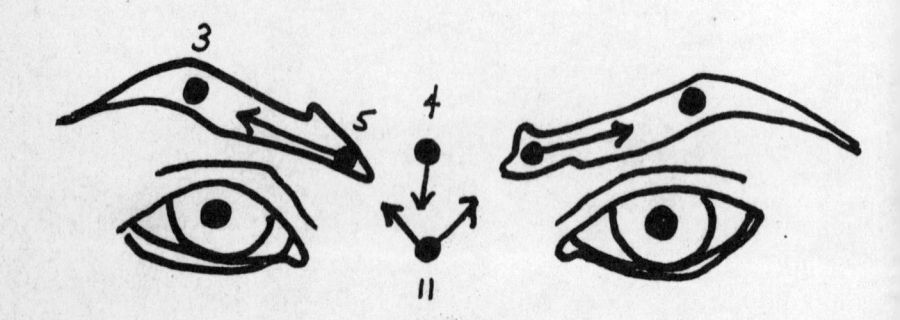

Areas stimulated: *Points 4, 11, 5, 3.*

Point 4. Between your eyebrows.

Point 11. On the bridge of your nose.

Point 5. At the inner corners of your eyebrows.

Point 3. Center of your eyebrows.

Massage Points 4, 11, 5 and 3 in the regular manner for 7 seconds at maximum pressure. Then using both index fingers, simultaneously tap over Points 4 and 11 for 1 minute.

UNDER EYE LIFT

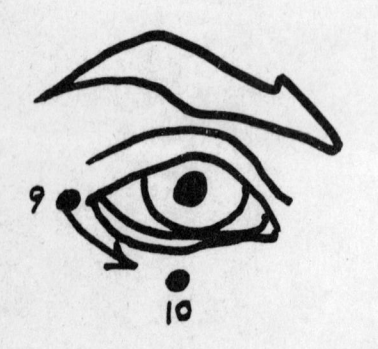

Areas stimulated: *Points 9, 10.*

Point 9. Outer corners of your eyes.

Point 10. Notch in the center of your lower eye socket.

Gently tap each point for 1 minute and/or massage in the regular manner for 7 seconds at maximum pressure.

EYES: OUTER CORNERS

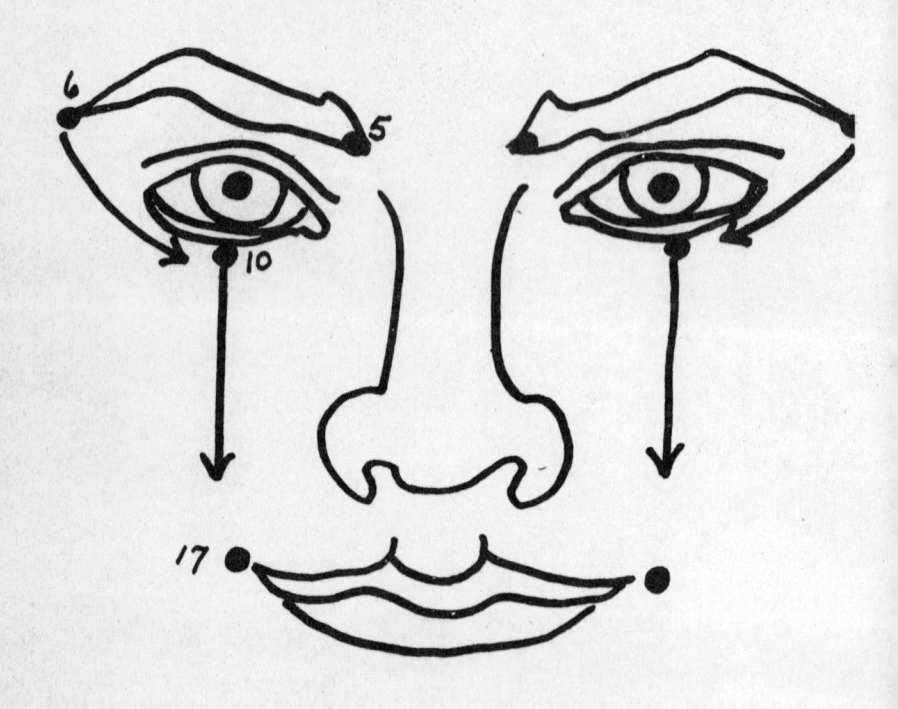

Mini-Lifts for Problem Areas

Areas Stimulated: *Points 5, 6, 10, 17.*

Point 5. At the inner corners of your eyebrows.

Point 6. Outer end of your eyebrows.

Point 10. Notch in the lower center of your eye socket, on the bone.

Point 17. Just outside the corners of your mouth.

Massage the above points in the regular manner for 7 seconds at maximum pressure. Then lightly tap Point 5 for 1 minute.

CHEEK LIFT

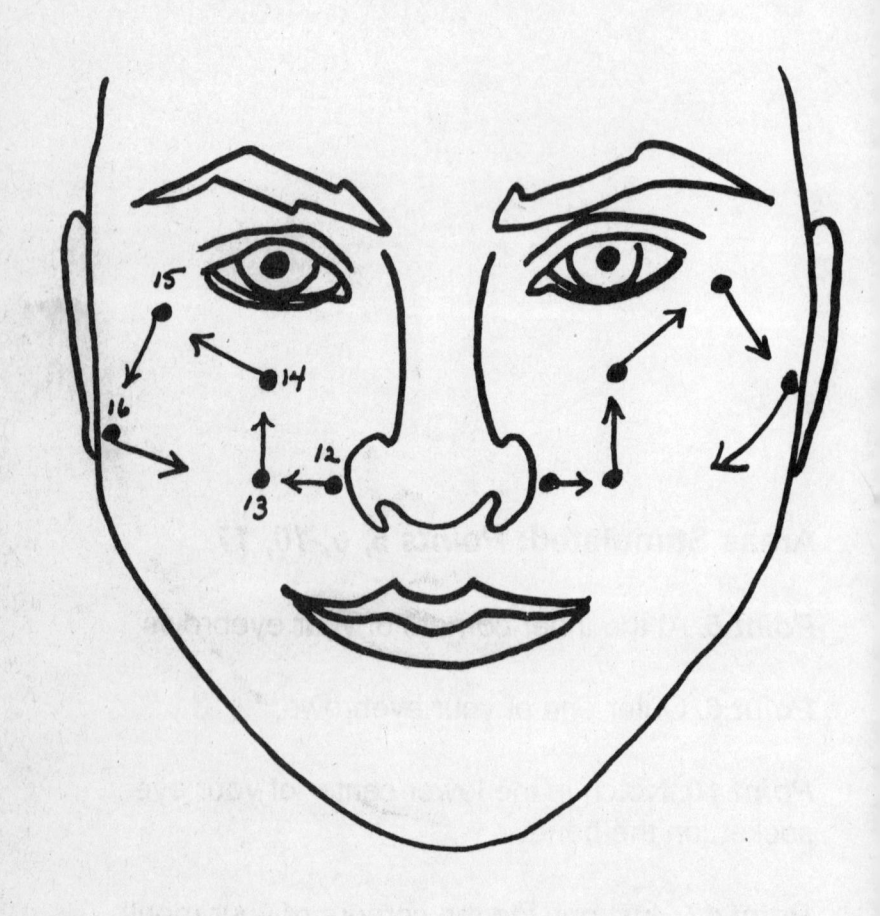

Areas stimulated: *Points 12, 13, 14, 15, 16.*

Point 12. On either side of the flare of your nostrils.

Point 13. Directly below the center of your eye at a line about even with the flare of your nostrils.

Point 14. About an inch below your eye, on a line about even with the midpoint of your nose.

Point 15. About one and one-half inches from the corner of your eye on a line that runs from the corner of your eye to the corner of your jawbone.

Point 16. About an inch in front of your ear.

Massage the above points in the regular manner for 7 seconds at maximum pressure, then lightly tap over the points for 1 minute each, making sure your jaw is relaxed.

UPPER LIP LINES

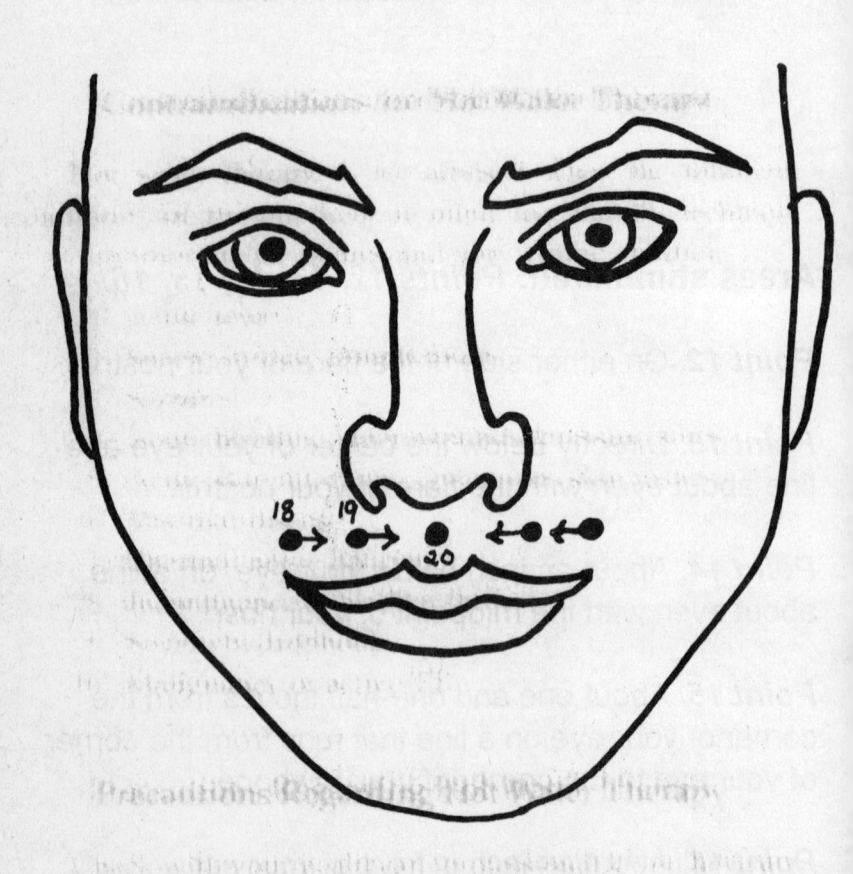

Areas stimulated: *Points 18, 19, 20.*

Point 18. One half-inch above the outside corners of your mouth.

Point 19. Under your nostrils, midway between the nostrils and your upper lip.

Point 20. In the nasolabial cleft, midway between your nose and upper lip.

Massage the above points in your regular manner for 7 seconds at maximum pressure. Then lightly tap over the same points for 30 seconds

MOUTH CORNERS
(Marionette Lines)

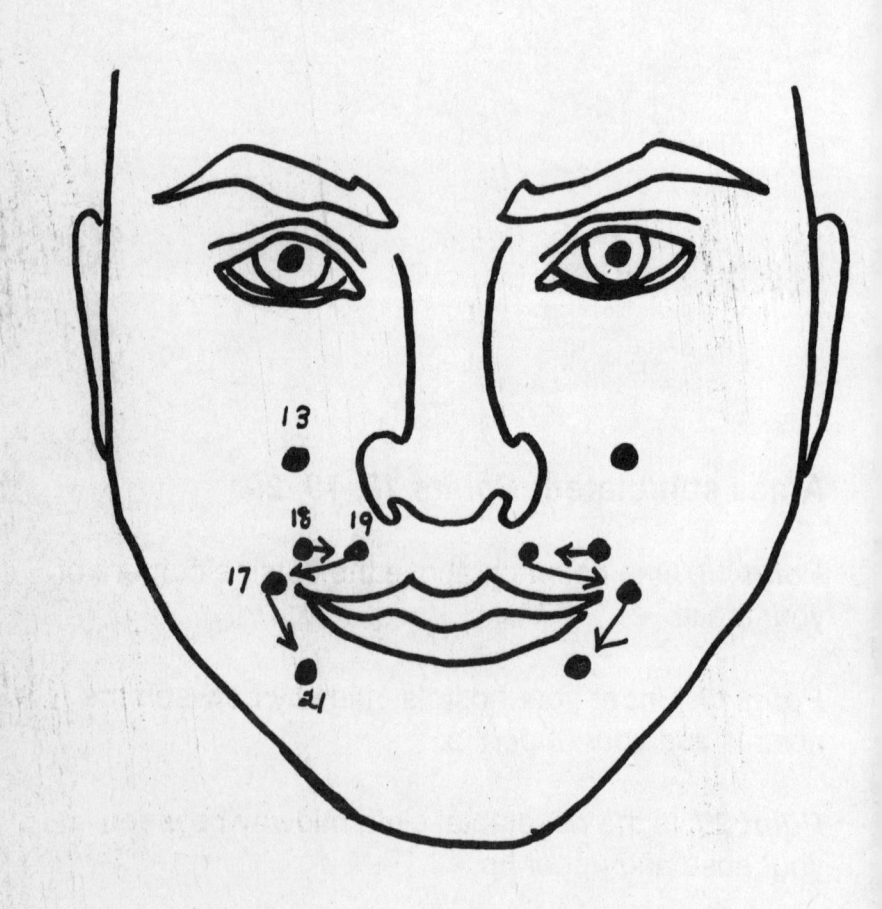

Areas stimulated: *Points 18, 19, 17, 21, 13.*

Point 18. One-half inch above the outside corners of your mouth.

Point 19. Under your nostrils, midway between the nostrils and your upper lip.

Point 17. Slightly outside the corners of your mouth.

Point 21. Midway between your lower lip and chin, about one-half inch from the corners of your mouth.

Point 13. Directly below the center of your eyes at a line about even with the flare of your nostrils.

Massage the above points in your regular manner for 7 seconds at maximum pressure. Then lightly tap over the same points, circling the mouth, tapping for 30 extra seconds over Point 13.

NASOLABIAL FOLDS
(Lines running from the sides of the nose to the outside corners of the mouth)

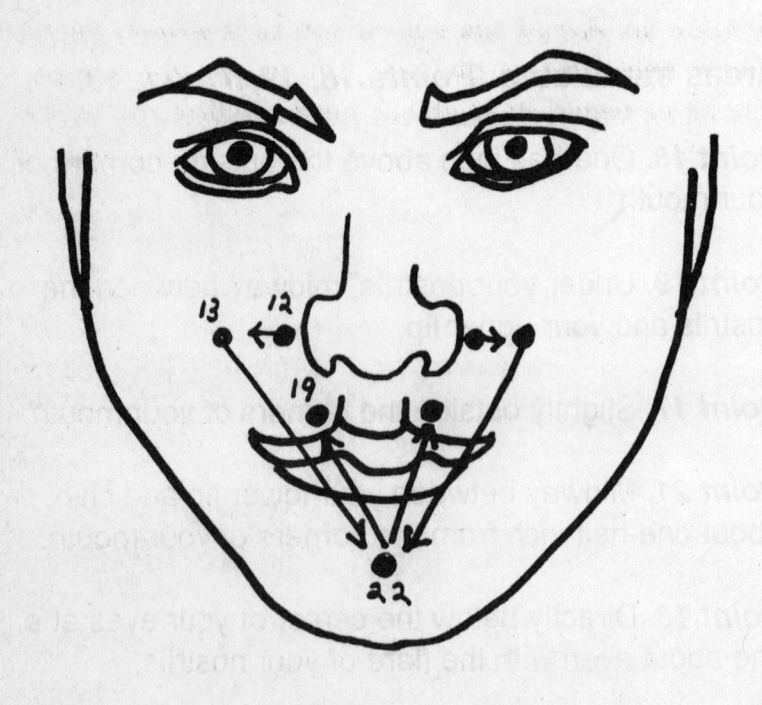

Areas stimulated: *Points 12, 13, 22, 19.*

Point 12. Found on either side of the flare of your nostrils.

Point 13. Directly below the center of your eyes at a line about even with the flare of your nostrils.

Point 22. In the center of your chin.

Point 19. Under your nostrils, midway between your nostrils and upper lip.

Massage the above points in your regular manner for 7 seconds at maximum pressure. Then lightly tap over the same points for 30 extra seconds.

106　　　　　　　　　Facelift　Naturally

CHIN LIFT

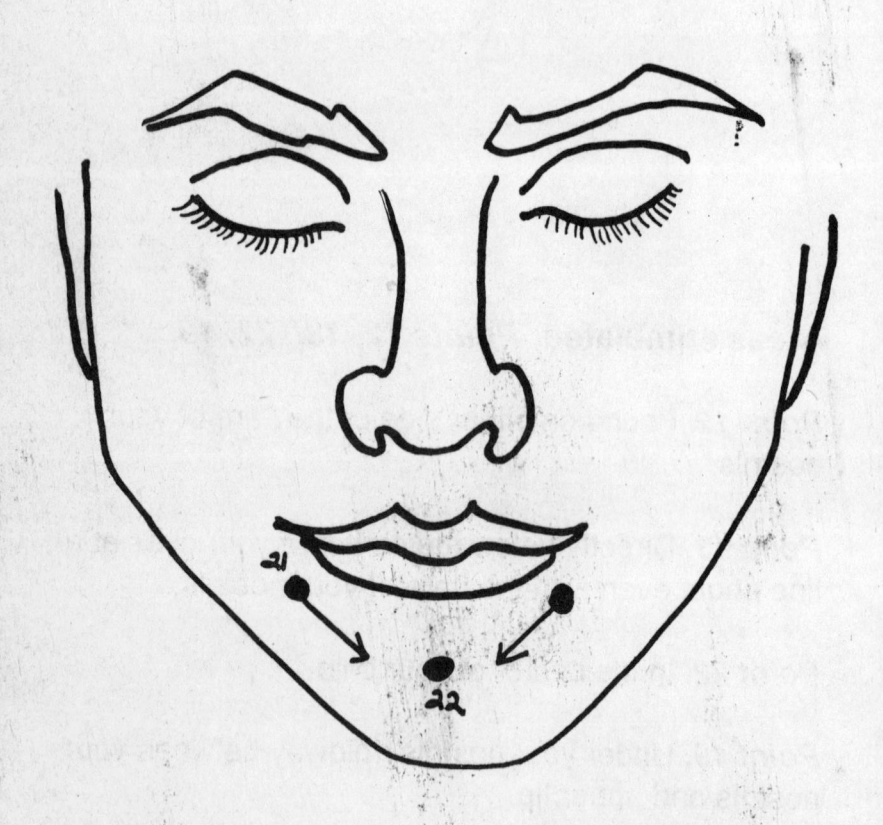

Areas stimulated: *Points 21, 22.*

Point 21. Midway between your lower lip and chin, about one-half inch from the corners of your mouth.

Point 22. In the center of your chin.

Massage the above points in your regular manner for 7 seconds at maximum pressure, then lightly tap over the same area for 30 seconds.

DOUBLE CHIN AND NECK LIFT

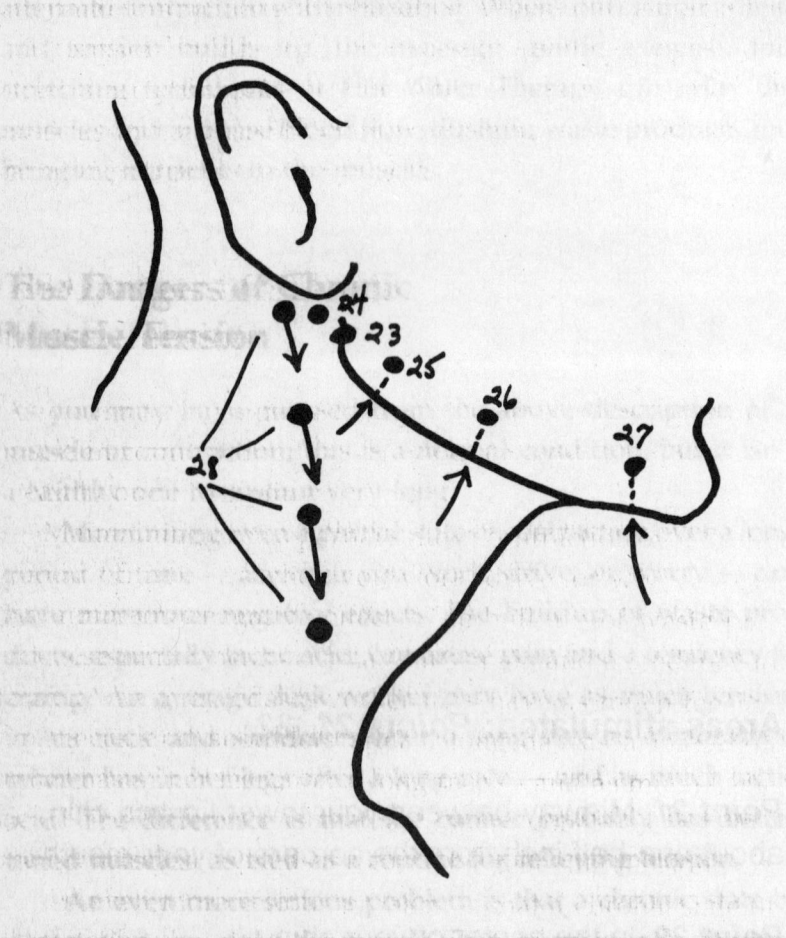

The points are stimulated as in the Facelift. As neck points they are held for only 3 seconds at maximum pressure, except for Point 30 which is stimulated for 7 seconds.

Areas stimulated: Points 23, 24, 25, 26, 27, 28, 29, 30.

Point 23. Found directly below your ears in the notch in the back of your jawbone.

Point 24. Behind the back edge of your jawbone on your neck directly under your ears.

Point 25. Under your jawbone in a deep depression about 1 inch from the back corner.

Point 26. The depression about halfway behind the back corner of your jawbone and your chin.

Point 27. Located directly behind your chin, Point 27 is best stimulated with your knuckle.

Point 28. Actually an area running along the muscle from the back of your ear to the "vee" at the base of your throat.
It is divided into four points:
    A) Located at the base of your ear.
    B) One-quarter of the distance to the "vee".
    C) One-half the distance to the "vee".
    D) Three-quarters of the distance to the "vee".
Point 28 requires a modified pinching motion.

(continued on next page)

110   Facelift   Naturally

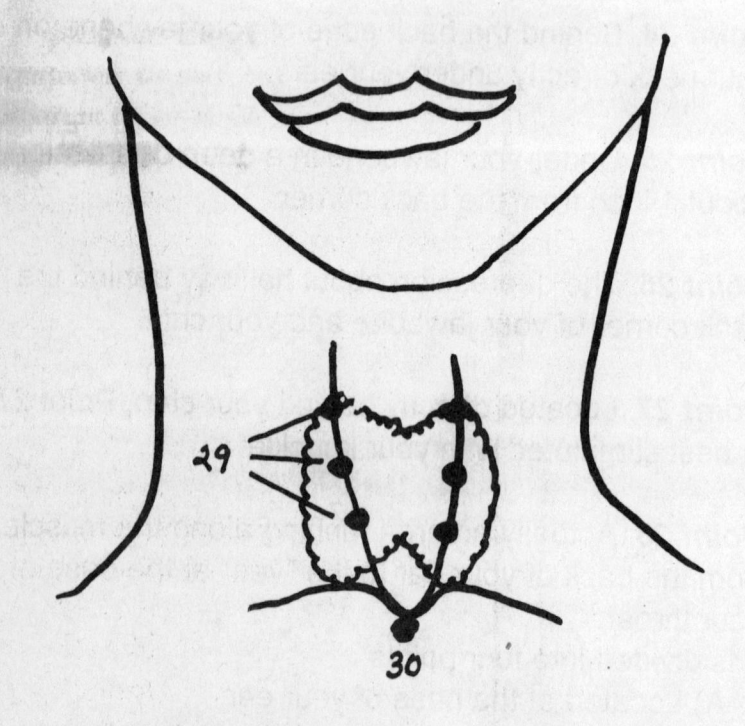

29
30

Point 29. At either side of your windpipe, over your thyroid gland, about one-half the distance down your neck. *Point 29 is either vibrated with 3 fingers of each hand or quickly and gently squeezed and released 3 times.*

Point 30. Located in the notch of the bone in the "vee" at the base of your neck. Remember to hold maximum pressure for the count of 7.

For serious neck lifting, see also The Back of the Neck & Scalp Massage, Points 1A - 8A, pages 88-89.

112   *Facelift Naturally*

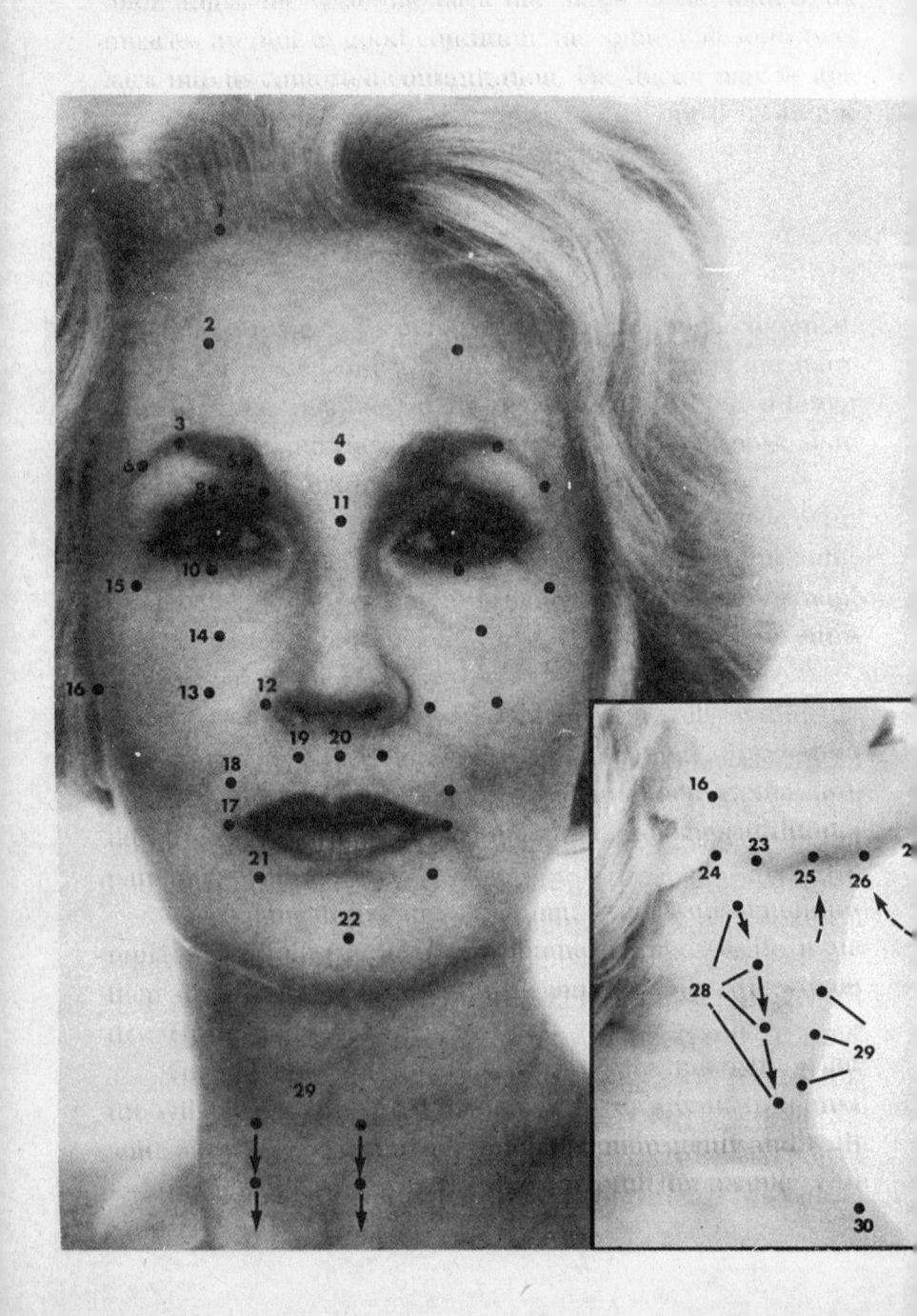

10. A FABULOUS FACE (HINTS FOR!)

1. **Drink 6 to 10, 8 ounce glasses of water a day.** Distilled or bottled is best. This does not include coffee, tea, soup, juice or sodas. Only water is water. Adequate water will provide the moisture needed to "plump" your skin.

2. **Hydrate your skin from the outside** with moisture-gathering ingredients: urea, lactic acid, NaPCA (sodium pyrrolidone carboxylate), also ingredients such as honey and aloe are natural moisturizers.

3. **Seal in moisture with oils that contain essential fatty acids.** Cold pressed vegetable oils, such as avocado, olive, castor, almond and evening primrose are excellent, among others. Jojoba oil is very similar to your skin's own oil in that it is both waxy and oily. Cold pressed oils can be found at your health food store.

4. **Get enough sleep.** Without it, no one has a fabulous face.

5. **Exfoliate during or after cleansing.** Remove your skin's dead outer layer daily. Dead skin cells build up every 24 hours. Removing them stimulates new cell growth and clears the way for nutrient absorption. Cleansing with oatmeal, cornmeal, fine grained sea salt or sugar will do the job. Just dampen your face and lightly rub your exfoliant over your skin without adding pressure. Let the exfoliant do the work for one minute. Excellent also, after cleansing, are preparations that include green papaya extract (papain), or bromelain, plant enzymes that dissolve away the dead skin. Steer clear of exfoliants that require you to rub them off of your skin. Your skin can be too easily stretched or irritated in this way.

6. **Eat plenty of raw fruits and vegetables.**

7. **Wear a sunscreen (SPF 15)** when going into the sunlight. Experts say that the ultraviolet rays of the sun may be responsible for 90 percent of all wrinkles.

8. **Don't smoke.** Smoking destroys the vitamin C that keeps your collagen fibers attached to your skin and your skin attached to the fatty pad underneath. After thirty, a smoker ages much more rapidly than a non-smoker.

9. **Sleep on your back,** or you will wake up looking like your rumpled sheets.

10. **Take care not to over express yourself** by emoting lines into your face. While you are on the phone, have a mirror nearby and check yourself.

11. **Exercise regularly.** Whether it is aerobic dance, yoga, basketball or a walk after dinner, exercise brings blood and nutrients to the skin and can even add thickness to aging skin. It also revives the elasticity.

12. **Practice your Facelift Naturally and you will have a fabulous face.**

Personal Notes

Date I started **FACELIFT NATURALLY** _____

In _____ days I noticed:

In _____ week(s) I noticed:

In one month I noticed:

My maintenance requires _____ day(s) a week.

Comments
    From Family:

    From Friends:

Those who asked or said:

    "Did you change your hair or something?"

    "Have you been on vacation?"

    "Are the kids on vacation?"

    "Are you in love?"

    "You're looking really good lately!"

Those who actually announced:

    "You've had some work done-- I know it!"

Index

A

Abdomen 47
Achilles tendon 81
Acupressure system 23
Acupuncture 17
Adrenal glands 79
Almond oil 113
Aloe 113
Arms, relaxation of 37, 39
Attitude
   during ritual 27
   toward aging 16
Avocado oil 113

B

Backbone. *See* vertebra(ae).
Balance
   of energy 28
   sense of 29
Bath 51
Bilateral 23
Bladder 81
Body
   points on 27, 73 - 82
   pressing from core of 20
   sensations, transmissions
     in 17
   stimulation of 82
   tone and function of 17

Bonus points.
   See body points.
Breathing
   at maximum pressure
     27, 29
   deeply 27
Bromelain 114
Brow, points 47 - 49
   See also mini-lift(s).
"Bubbles" 65

C

Castor oil 113
Cervical vertebra(-ae).
   See vertebrae.
Cheek(s)
   firming, plumping points
     for 56 - 59
   "roses in" 56
   tapping over 59
   See also mini-lift(s).
Chin
   double. *See* neck,
     mini-lift(s).
   plumping, tightening,
     toning, points on 62
   See also mini-lift(s).
Circular motion massage 36
   Point 3A and 37
   Point 2B, 3B and 76, 77

Scalp and 40
Circulation, around eyes
  to scalp, neck, face 51
Colds, congestion, hoarseness 64, 65, 70
Collagen 114
Cornmeal 114
Crowsfeet 50
Cup, as pressure point 21
Current, balancing of 28

D

Digestion, improvement sluggish 17
Direct pressure. *See* pressure.
Dizziness 61
Do-in 17

E

Ear(s), massaging behind points, sensitivity 64 - 65
Elbow point 76
Emergency point 61
Energy
  eye points and 51
  from hands 27
  from scalp to face 43, 45
  increase of 17
  into forehead 49
  pressure points and 17
  quick 32

rebalancing of 17
systemic 69
to face 58, 63
to mouth 62
to neck and head 70
Enzymes, plant 114
Essential fatty acids 113
Evening primrose oil 113
Exfoliate, how to 114
Eye(s)
  bags 63
  corners (outer) 52
  energy to 50 - 54
  general relief for 51- 53
  how to touch 55
  points on sockets 52 - 53
  tapping around 54
  See also mini-lift(s).
Eyebrows
  between 49
  points on 49, 50
  relaxation of 49
Eyelids
  droopy 52
  See also mini-lift(s).
Eyestrain relief 53

F

Face
  changes to 15, 16
  channels to 47, 63 - 70
  circulation, warmth to 48
  contours, restoration of 56

delineation of 43
fabulous, hints for 113-115
points on 42, 47-62, 112
wrinkles, sagging 16
See also facelift.

Facelift
maintenance of 71
maximum pressure for, Four Pound Rule 45
points for 42 - 70
results, best, when to expect 44, 71
sections, working in 44
sequence for 43 - 44
session, length of 44
timing 46

Fainting, point for 61

Fingers. See also thumb(s).
as extensions 20
contact, during ritual 23 - 26
crossing, doubling 20
index 20, 32, 68, 77
middle 20, 68
pads of 19, 23, 25
pressure 15. See also maximum pressure.
one, lifting with 18
stress in 65
three 75
vibrating with 69, 111

Fingernails 23

Fingerprinting 19
Food, absorption of 80
Foot point 81
Forehead points 47- 49.
See also mini-lift(s).
Four Pound Rule 45
Fruits, raw 114

G

Gall bladder 47

H

Hairline points 84
Hand(s) points 77, 78
tension in 39, 51, 54, 59, 62, 82
warming, energizing 27, 45, 74, 83
Head, master point 77
releasing 71
warmth to 34, 48
Headache, migraine, relieving 17, 47, 48, 51
Honey 113

I

Indentation as pressure point 21
Insomnia relief 48
Intestine, large, points 56, 77

Index

J

Jaw(-bone) tension, relaxing, points on 58, 63
Jojoba 113

K

Kidney 81
Knuckle(s) 20, 67, 79

L

Lactic acid 113
Lines
  fine 16
  mouth corners (marionette) 102 - 103
  over emoting and 115
  smoking and 114
  ultraviolet rays and 114
  upper cheeks and eyes 56 - 57
  See also wrinkles.
Lip(s) points. *See* mini-lifts.
Liver 47
Lumbar vertebra(-ae). *See* vertebra(-ae).

M

Marionette lines. *See* lines. *See also* mini-lift(s).
Massage, daily 71 - 74
  neck, back of 38 - 39
  neuromuscular 17
  scalp 32, 34, 40
  technique for 19 - 20, 23 - 26
  See also circular motion; direct pressure; modified pinching motion; pivoting, pulsating.
Maximum pressure
  face, neck and 23 - 26
  options 35 - 36
  pleasure-pain and 23
  procedure for 24 - 25
Medulla 32
Meridian
  bladder 81
  disruption of 71 - 72
  gall bladder 47
  kidney 81
  large intestine 56, 77
  liver 47
  network, pressure points and 17
Metabolism 69
Migraine. *See* headache.
Mini-Lifts
  brow 84 - 85
  cheek 98 - 99
  chin 106 - 107
    double 108 - 111
  eye(s)
    between 92 - 96

Index

corners, outer 96 - 97
general 86 - 89
lid, upper 90 - 91
under eye 94 - 95
lip, upper 100 - 101
marionette lines (mouth corners 102 - 103
neck 108 - 111
nasolabial folds 104-105
Modified pinching motion. *See* pinching.
Moisturizers 113
Mouth 60 - 62
See also mini-lift(s).

N

NaPCA 113
Nasolabial
cleft 61, 101
folds 56
See also mini-lift(s).
Nausea point 61
Neck
back of, points on 27, 38 - 39, 70, 71
front of, points on 64 - 69, 108 - 111
master point to 77
maximum pressure on 29
See also mini-lift(s).
Nose, bridge of
point on 53, 92 - 93

Notch as pressure point 21
Nourishment distribution point 75

O

Oatmeal 114
Oils, cold pressed 113
Olive oil 113
Organs, internal point 75

P

Pad(s) of fingers, thumb(s)
contacting, pressing with 19, 22 - 26
fingerprinting with 19
"Piggyback" 20
Pain
avoidance of 23, 24
insensitivity to 45
pressing out 34
reflecting 24
Papain 114
Papaya, green 114
Pinching, modified motion, points stimulated by 68, 77, 81
Pivoting 34, 35
Point 2A and 37
Points 2B and 76
Pleasure, pressure and 23
Points. *See* pressure points.
Pressure

Index

direct 35, 46
extra 20
finger 17
how to apply 22-25
maximum. *See* maximum pressure.
  pleasure of 23 - 24
  releasing 24
Pressure points
  as transmitters 17
  avoiding 23
  bilateral 23
  bonus. *See* body.
  facial. *See* facelift.
  function of 17
  how to find 21
  how to touch 19 - 20
  location of, general 17
  meridians and 17
  neck, back of and scalp 31 - 34, 88 - 89, 111
  1A - 8A. *illus.* 42,112
  1A 32, 40, 89
  2A 32, 34, 89
  3A 33, 34, 89
  4A 32, 33, 89
  5A 38, 39, 89
  6A 38, 39, 89
  7A 38, 39, 89
  8A 38, 39, 89
  1 - 30. *illus.* 42, 112
  1 47
  2 48, 84 - 85
  3 49, 84 - 87, 90 - 93
  4 49, 54, 84 - 85, 92 - 93
  5 50, 85 - 87, 93 - 93, 96 - 97
  6 50, 86 - 87, 96 - 97
  7 21, 51, 54, 86 - 87
  8 52, 86 - 87, 90 - 91
  9 52, 54, 86 - 87, 94 - 95
  10 53, 54, 86 - 87, 94 - 97
  11 53, 54, 93 - 93
  12 56, 59, 98 - 99, 104 - 105
  13 21, 59, 98 - 99, 102 - 105
  14 57, 59, 98 - 99
  15 57, 59, 98 - 99
  16 58, 59, 98 - 99
  17 60, 96 - 97, 102 -103
  18 60,100 - 103
  19 61,100 - 105
  20 61,100 - 101
  21 62,102 - 103, 106 - 107
  22 62,104 - 107
  23 63, 108 - 109
  24 64, 108 - 109
  25 65, 108 - 109
  26 66, 108 - 109
  27 67, 108 - 109
  28 68, 108 - 109
  29 69, 108 - 111
  30 70, 108 - 111
  1B 75
  2B 76
  3B 77

Index

4B 78
5B 79
6B 80
7B 81
Pulsating, pulsing 31, 36
   Point 4A and 37

R

Rejuvenation
   program and 17, 71
   messages of 17
   pressure points and 17
   time needed for 71
Ritual
   as second nature 18
   attitude during 27
   basis of 17
   breathing during. *See* breathing.
   how to begin 27
   repetition of 71
   results, benefits
      changes due to 15 - 18

S

Scalp massage. *See* massage.
Scarring 71
Sea salt 114
Sensitivity
   areas of 34, 49, 63, 65
   pressing out 34
   tapping and 59
Shiatsu 17
Shoulders, kneading of 43, 71
Sinus relief 51 - 54, 56 - 57
Skin
   body points for. *See* bonus points.
   "brown spots" on 16
   collagen 116
   contact during massage 23 - 25
   exfoliation of 114
   hydration of 113
   injury, irritation, of 20, 23, 24, 26, 45, 74
   memory of 72
   oils for 113
   plumping of 56, 113
   rubbing 25
   softer, smoother 16
   stretching 35, 114
   ultraviolet protection of 114
   youthful 16
   See also thyroid.
Skull, points. *See points 1A - 4A.*
Slant board 51
Sleep 115
Smoking 114
Squeezing. *See* pinching.
Stomach point 75
Stress. *See* tension.

Sugar 114
Sunscreen 114
Surgery, lifts 15, 71

T

Tap(-ping)
 brow area 49
 cheeks 59
 eye(s) 54
 how to 49
 mouth 62
 chin 62
Technique, basic in brief 26
 See also circular motion;
  pinching motion (modified); pivoting; pulsating;
  vertebrae, cervical.
Tension, areas, releasing
 29, 39, 49, 50, 51,
 52, 53, 54
Thumb(s) 32, 40, 63, 65,
 66, 68
 pads, balls of 19, 26, 51
Thyroid points 69
Touch, how, where to 19 - 26
 See also four pound rule.

U

Ultraviolet 114
Urea 113

V

"Vee" point 70
Vegetables 114
Vertebra(-ae)
 cervical points,
  technique for 38 - 39
 lumbar points 79, 80
Vibrating
 Point 29 (thyroid) and
  69, 111
Vision, points to clear 51-53
Vitamin C 114

W

Water 113
Weight control 69
Windpipe 69, 111
Wrinkles, heavy 71
 See also lines.
Wrist point 78

Y

Yawning, as release 28, 39

The Author

Born in 1940, Julia Busch now 50 plus, has no desire to grow old or "age gracefully".

Always interested in health, well-being and beauty in its broadest sense, Julia has researched the subject since the early 1970s, most recently contributing to *Let's Live* magazine and *Inner Self*. She acquired training in aromatherapy, established Anti-Aging Press, a publishing house, and co-hosts "Youthfully Yours" on Talk America sharing information on holistic care and "youth extension". *Facelift Naturally*, her first book, is now available worldwide. Her audio cassette, *Youth and Skin Secrets*, encompasses a wide variety of anti-aging topics.

Her first love was the arts. She studied voice and opera at Juilliard School of Music, and then sculpture and art history at the University of Miami, Florida, and at Columbia University. In the 1970s she authored *A Decade of Sculpture: The Media of the 1960s*, now a reference book. She has taught drawing, sculpture and painting, researched plastic as an art form, and contributed to books on the same subject.

Also in Orient Paperbacks

Herbal Beauty Care
Parvesh Handa

The book gives hundreds of recipes for every kind of beauty preparation — cleansing creams and face masks, conditioners for your hands, neck, feet and knees, lotions and oils for bath and for massage, skin tonics, antiwrinkle creams, astringents, moisturisers and toners, hair conditioners and colourants, deodorants and powders — all based on fruits, vegetables, herbs and spices.

Parvesh Handa is a well known beautician-columnist who has a long experience in using honey, curd, milk, lemon, vinegar and other natural substances as beauty aids. In this book she has also given simple exercises and diets based on natural foods to keep you fresh and trim.

"The book meets the burgeoning demand for cosmetics made of herbs and such things."

Amrita Bazar Patrika

Illustrated   pp176   Rs 60.00

Also in Orient Paperbacks

Walk Slim
The easy way to lose weight in 30 days
Les Snowdon and Maggice Humphreys

Walk Slim to melt any excess fat away, to tone up your body and have more energy and vitality than you have ever had before!

Walk Slim to get slim and stay slim, even if other fitness and weight loss routines have failed.

Easier than aerobics, swimming or jogging, walking is the easiest and the most effective way to lose weight and become fit. The almost 'forgotten art' walking is fast becoming the exercise of the times — and just about anyone can do it, young and old.

According to the World Health Organisation, *"A walker loses weight, lowers cholesterol, reduces conditions associated with hypertension, slows the ageing process; increases strength, flexibility and balance, strengthens bones and increases stamina".*

Illustrated   pp192   Rs 130.00

Also in Orient Paperbacks

Shahnaz Husain's Beauty Book

"Internationally famous — she is an established name in Skin and Hair care."
The New York Times

"She is spreading the rich herbal heritage of India around the world."
Guardian

"Fabulous and fascinating."
Barbara Cartland, London

"Asia's Helena Rubinstein."
Espirit, Germany

"Shahnaz Husain combines ancient herbal remedies wtih scientific techniques very effectively".
Washington Post, USA

"Shahnaz Husain is India's sacred goddess of beauty."
Jardin Desmodes, Paris

"Internationally recognized authority on herbs... a Phenomenal success."
B.B.C.

26 Colur Pic., Illustrated   pp184   Rs 175.00

Available at all bookshops or by V.P.P.

Orient Paperbacks
Madarsa Road, Kashmere Gate, Delhi-110 006